THE
REAL
FACE
OF
ATHEISM

Other books by Ravi Zacharias

Can Man Live without God

Cries of the Heart: Bringing God Near When He Feels So Far

Deliver Us from Evil: Restoring the Soul in a Disintegrating Culture

I, Isaac, Take Thee, Rebekah: Moving from Romance to Lasting Love

Is Your Church Ready? Motivating Leaders to Live an Apologetic Life (coeditor with Norman Geisler)

Jesus Among Other Gods: The Absolute Claims of the Christian Message

Light in the Shadow of Jihad: The Struggle for Truth

The Lotus and the Cross: Jesus Talks with Buddha

Recapture the Wonder

Sense and Sensuality: Jesus Talks with Oscar Wilde on the Pursuit of Pleasure

Who Made God? And Answers to Over 100 Other Tough Questions of Faith (coeditor with Norman Geisler)

THE
REAL
FACE
OF
ATHEISM

RAVI ZACHARIAS

BakerBooks
Grand Rapids, Michigan

© 1990, 2004 by Ravi Zacharias

Published by Baker Books
a division of Baker Publishing Group
P.O. Box 6287, Grand Rapids, MI 49516-6287
www.bakerbooks.com

The Real Face of Atheism is the revised and updated edition of *A Shattered Visage: The Real Face of Atheism* (Grand Rapids: Baker Books, 1990).

Fourth printing, December 2006

Printed in the United States of America

Library of Congress Cataloging-in-Publication Data
Zacharias, Ravi K.
    The real face of atheism / Ravi Zacharias.
        p.   cm.
    Rev. ed. of: A shattered visage. 1990.
    Includes bibliographical references.
    ISBN 10: 0-8010-6511-9 (pbk.)
    ISBN 978-0-8010-6511-8 (pbk.)
    1. Atheism. 2. Apologetics. I. Zacharias, Ravi K. Shattered visage. II. Title.
BT1212.Z33 2004
239′.7—dc22   2004011991

Scripture is taken from the HOLY BIBLE, NEW INTERNATIONAL VERSION®. NIV®. Copyright © 1973, 1978, 1984 by International Bible Society. Used by permission of Zondervan. All rights reserved.

Scripture marked KJV is taken from the King James Version of the Bible.

Song lyrics on page 151 from "Finally Home" words and music by Don Wyrtzen © 1971 Singspiration Music (ASCAP) (Administered by Brentwood-Benson Music Publishing, Inc.) All Rights Reserved. Used by permission.
Reprinted by special permission of Brentwood-Benson Music Publishing, Inc.

Song lyrics excerpt on page 165 from "Dear Mr. Jesus" words and music by Richard Klender © 1985 Klenco Music / Songtracker.com (ASCAP) http://www.DayOfTheChild.org / Used by permission / all rights reserved / international copyright secured.

To my dear friend
"D.D." Davis,
who in life and
death demonstrated
to me more powerfully
than any argument could
that "man shall not live by bread alone"

Contents

ACKNOWLEDGMENTS

There have been many who have helped me in getting this manuscript ready for publication. I would like to thank Drs. David Lalka, Norman Geisler, Ramesh Richard for their critiques and constructive input. In this revised edition I am deeply grateful to Danielle DuRant, my research assistant, who meticulously worked through every page to make this manuscript more complete, including developing study questions for each chapter. For all her hours spent behind a computer I am grateful to my executive assistant, Nancy Bevers. But most of all, no one has given up more nor had more of a share in this accomplishment than my wife, Margie. I cannot gainsay her hard work in helping me. Last, but not least, my children insist that they have paid the price, too, by sacrificing many hours of play with their father, and they are right. My affectionate thanks to them also.

PREFACE
TO THE
REVISED EDITION

The idea for the approach I have taken came following an address I gave to a group of scientists at the Bell Labs in Holmdel, New Jersey. I addressed the subject "Why I Am Not an Atheist," a response to Bertrand Russell's *Why I Am Not a Christian*. The most telling aspect of that afternoon was the nature of the questions that were raised following the address. None of the questions bespoke the technical or scientific expertise that the audience represented. Rather, they all involved the heart-searching questions of men and women in pursuit of meaning in life.

I have found these same questions asked time and again in a variety of settings. After the intellectual smokescreen is cleared away, it is the felt reality of life's struggles within each individual that comes to the fore.

INTRODUCTION

Former presidential candidate and governor Alfred E. Smith told of the occasion when he was a member of a fishing party somewhere in New England. Devotion to their faith led him and a few members of the party to roll out of bed early on Sunday morning to take in a church service. As they tiptoed past their serenely slumbering mates, one of his friends, walking close behind him, heard one half-slumbering fellow mutter, "Wouldn't it be awful if it turned out they were right!"

It is common for many in their spiritual journey to ponder the veracity of their beliefs. The realities of life, however, powerfully reinforce the viability of faith in God. Even atheists confess in their writings that they have pondered the possibility of theism. For some, it becomes a lingering concern. Others, through various processes of argumentation, feel protected and quite secure within their unbelief. Nevertheless, the jagged edges of reality keep cutting into their atheistic armor, rendering their philosophy very vulnerable. The existential undeniabilities of life find very few answers in a world that happened by accident. For those who are willing to seek earnestly the possibility of God's existence, this book has been written.

It has been said that, if one does not know the facts, argument is to no avail, and if one does know the facts, argument is unnecessary. Like all epigrams, this one also runs the risk of overgeneralization. But it does so while pointing out a vital truth. Facts are

13

indispensable to justify belief. And that is where a solution to the problem begins.

Bertrand Russell, who was no friend of religion and quite outspoken on such matters, argued heavily for the scientific outlook on life and described the scientific method. The first step, he said, consisted of observing the significant facts. But there, precisely, is a predicament—significant for what? There are an infinite number of facts out there that are in need of interpretation. How does one determine what is significant? Alfred E. Smith knew quite well that more was at stake than the privilege of sleeping in on Sunday morning. Rather, the question "What if they are right?" touches on the paradigm for all of life.

The selective process of fact finding, therefore, has not been easy. Communicating the Christian faith has become extremely complicated in our day. There are very few accepted beliefs any more. Never before has skepticism had such a brilliant halo around its head. There is a glory about "not knowing." A high premium is placed on the absence of conviction, and open-mindedness has become synonymous with intellectual sophistication.

But forgotten is the charge by the late English writer G. K. Chesterton that an open mind, like an open mouth, does have a purpose: to close upon something solid. Otherwise, it could become like a city sewer, rejecting nothing.

Christian communication is further impeded by the expectations of a world progressing at a staggering pace in every field of study. It seems as though to deal in spiritual matters, the Christian has to be an authority on every other subject, failing which, he is branded "escapist" or "unrealistic." Thus, science, philosophy, psychology, history, and virtually every other discipline affects religion. In a sense, this ought not to be surprising, because spiritual truth deals with the essence of life. For the theist, all truth is God's truth, and truth cannot be in conflict with itself.

The unpopularity of holding to convictions, coupled with the tall demand that one be able to touch on all pertinent subjects with authority, make it easy to see that any endeavor to write about atheism will be feeble. Hence I have accepted the caution of one of my professors, who said that many a book will never be written because the author wanted it to be the last word on the subject.

Knowing full well that this is neither the first nor the last word on the subject, my sincere hope is that the reader will recognize the importance of a book on the existence of God and seek the answer that can satisfy the mind and soul. Nothing is so valuable as the truth, and that is why Jesus said, "If the truth shall set you free, you shall be free, indeed." May that freedom be found through these pages.

It is often a temptation for those who think deeply to assume that all questions involve argumentation and academic skills at a high level of abstraction. In reality, however, judging by the often repeated questions, this is not so. Answers come our way in the nursery as well as in the science laboratory. This makes the tasks more manageable. It has, nevertheless, been challenging because some questions do present a serious intellectual obstacle.

I have tried to dispel the assumed power of logical arguments for atheism within a framework of argumentation. My purpose has been to clear the bushes so we can take a direct look at the counter-perspective of Christ. Those who prefer to read at a level of felt need may find some of the arguments to be weightier than they would desire. My hope is that they will stay with the argument until my illustrations capture the idea.

Others, who love the process of dialogue, might wish that the arguments were weightier than they are. My hope is that they will not fall into the trap of intellectualism and forget the splendor and power of simplicity. We are neither just brains floating around nor just hearts bouncing about.

In an effort to deal with some necessary academic material, I have included two appendixes. The first, "The Finger of Truth and the Fist of Reality," deals with the way philosophical ideas *do* come into our lives, apart from the classroom. The second one, "The Establishment of a Worldview," provides the conceptual foundation upon which the framework of truth can stand. Ideally, these appendixes should be earlier chapters in the book since they explain the process I have used in studying various concepts and arriving at conclusions. However, for many, that type of material would distract from the flow of thought; yet I hope the appendixes will not be ignored. At the appropriate junctures in the text I have recommended where they would be helpful. Those who so desire may digress to the appendixes at that point. Others may wish to continue in the text as it is. Whichever route is chosen, the material in the appendixes is particularly germane to my answers to the skeptic.

So with both mind and heart, let us engage in this quest for truth. Whether we carry a wallet or a purse, it is always a thrill to find suddenly a compartment with some forgotten money in it. May there be the discovery of some hidden gold in this book to lead us to the greatest treasure of all—God himself.

PART I

MAN

The Measure of All Things

I met a traveller from an antique land
Who said—"Two vast and trunkless legs of stone
Stand in the desert . . . Near them, on the sand,
Half sunk, a shattered visage lies, whose frown,
And wrinkled lip, and sneer of cold command,
Tell that the sculptor well those passions read
Which yet survive, stamped on these lifeless things,
The hand that mocked them, and the heart that fed;
And on the pedestal, these words appear:
My name is Ozymandias, King of Kings,
Look on my Works, ye Mighty, and despair!
Nothing beside remains. Round the decay
Of that colossal Wreck, boundless and bare
The lone and level sands stretch far away."

—Percy Bysshe Shelley, "Ozymandias"

I

MORTICIANS
OF THE ABSOLUTE

*The greatest question of our time is not communism
versus individualism; not Europe versus America; not
even the East versus West. It is whether men can live
without God.*

—Will Durant

On August 7, 1961, twenty-six-year-old Major Gherman Titov became the second Soviet cosmonaut to orbit the earth and return safely, climaxing a monumental feat for humankind. Some time later, speaking at the World's Fair and savoring his moment of glory, he recounted this experience, vouchsafed to a privileged few. Under a triumphalist pretext, he let it be known that, on his excursion into space, he hadn't seen God.[1] Upon hearing of this exuberant argument from silence, someone quipped, "Had he stepped out of his space-suit he would have!" Evidently reluctant to restrict the immediate gains of the moment to the disciplines directly involved in that endeavor, Titov attempted

19

to draw theological blood. Thus, one great step for science became, for him, an immensely greater leap in philosophy.

On Christmas Eve, 1968, three American astronauts were the first human beings to go around the "dark" side of the moon, away from the earth. Having fired their rockets, they were homebound on Apollo 8, and beheld our planet in a way that human eyes had never witnessed before. They saw Earth rise over the horizon of the moon, draped in a beauteous mixture of white and blue, bordered by the glistening light of the sun against the black void of space. And in the throes of this awe-inspiring experience they opened the pages of the book of Genesis and read for the world to hear, "In the beginning God created the heavens and the earth . . ."

Two similar experiences of awe and exhilaration; two diametrically opposed conclusions about the nature of the world. Such a chasm is quite understandable, for these two incidents carried into

> *"More consequences for life and action follow from the affirmation or denial of God than from any other basic question."*

space the most fundamentally debated question on earth: Does God exist? Has God created man, or has man created God? Is God indispensable to any cosmological explanation, or is he only a psychological necessity of men? Theism or atheism?

Several years ago, Encyclopedia Britannica published a fifty-five-volume series entitled *The Great Books of the Western World.* Mortimer Adler, a noted philosopher and legal scholar, was co-editor of this series, which marshaled the eminent thinkers of the western world and their writings on the most important ideas that have been studied and investigated over the centuries. This includes ideas in law, science, philosophy, history, theology, and love that have shaped the minds and destinies of people. These essays are assembled for comparison and contrast. Very striking to the observant reader is that the longest essay is on God. When Mr. Adler was asked by a reviewer why this theme merited such protracted coverage, his answer was uncompromising. "Because," said he, "more consequences for life and action follow from the affirmation or denial of God than from any other basic question."[2]

Even the most unsympathetic individual toward things religious will not want to contend with Adler's conclusion. Nothing, absolutely nothing, has a more direct bearing on the moral choices made by individuals or the purposes pursued by society than belief or disbelief in God. Personal and national destinies are inextricably bound to this issue. It is not accidental that the key issues of the day that are felt with deep emotion and conviction, whether it be the issue of sexual orientation and practice, or life in the fetal stage, sooner or later filter down to whether there is a God, and if so, has he spoken?

It is not surprising, therefore, that Stephen Hawking concluded his book *A Brief History of Time* asserting this question to be the most significant factor in the human equation. Hawking, who holds Newton's chair as Lucasian professor of Mathematics at Cambridge University, brilliantly laid out his view of the universe and ended with a humble assertion: the one question in need of an answer is the question of God. Science, with all of its strident gains, must still remain contented to describe the "what" of human observations. Only God can answer the "why."[3]

On the issue of God's existence, testifying to both the intellectual depth and pragmatic breadth of the subject, intellectual giants through the centuries have lined both sides of the fence, holding tenaciously to their own view and passionately rejecting the opposite. Brilliant minds such as Bertrand Russell and David Hume have severely castigated the intellectual credibility of theism. Yet, other great philosophical and scientific thinkers, such as Jonathan Edwards and Blaise Pascal, have firmly and unblushingly held the theistic worldview. Scientists and philosophers continue to debate the issue today. It is, then, utter folly to maintain, as some do, that informed minds have eschewed the idea of God, and that only the pre-scientific, unquestioning, antiquated, or simple-minded have succumbed to this belief, through fear or ignorance. Bertrand Russell's assertion, in his conceptual critique of Christianity, that all religion is born out of fear, is a weak and unthinking criticism of the subject. It is no more true than if one were to say that all irreligion is born out of fearlessness. Caricatures such as this make for a poor philosophical starting point, and end up in false psychological theories. In life, it is not uncommon to meet many intensely self-assured people who are devoutly religious. And, it is also not uncommon to meet some equally insecure people, embattled by manifold fears, who are devoutly irreligious.

To further compound the issues surrounding the debate about God's existence, both sides have made inductive and deductive mistakes. Any student of history or science is quite familiar with the tragic display of power and ignorance when the mathematician, physicist, and astronomer Galileo was forced by the Inquisition in 1633 to recant his support of the Copernican theory of the solar system. But many of these students do not know that this censorious autocracy, which the church arrogated to itself, was not based on any biblical pronouncement, but rather, on a fallacious assumption from the teachings of the second-century Greek astronomer and mathematician, Ptolemy.[4] He postulated that the earth lay at the center of the universe with the sun, moon, and other planets revolving around it. The ecclesiastical hierarchy of the day espoused this Aristotelian-Ptolemaic cosmology, with its erroneous conclusion, as being the worldview of the Bible. The Bible, in fact, states nothing of the kind. Critics have never allowed the church to forget the Galileo blunder, and have consistently expelled it from the halls of academic credibility.

On the other side of the fence, supporters of the materialistic, non-theistic worldview have had their share of error-ridden deductions. Their Galileo blunder was the Piltdown hoax. Doctoral candidates wrote numerous dissertations on the Piltdown Man in support of the theory of evolution. These fossilized skull fragments, discovered in Sussex, England, in 1913, supposedly argued for an advanced hominid. Although at that time believed to be the earliest European human remains, it was proved a hoax forty years later, bringing the scientific community great embarrassment.

It is not without reason that philosophers, scientists, theologians, and others have written prolifically on the matter of God's existence, and our libraries are crowded with assumptions and deductions, ad nauseum. How may anyone, then, hope to find valid answers to their gnawing questions on this subject?

There are many approaches from which this issue can be studied. We could view it scientifically, historically, philosophically, existentially, or pragmatically. Each avenue lends its own distinctive strength. Each can tender volumes to the argument, with or without relevance. For the purpose of this brief presentation, the challenge presented to atheism is one that will touch more weightily upon the existential struggle of humankind, for in the words of Max Weber, the German sociologist, "man embraces religion at the point of meaning." However, while studying it from this vantage point, I will also attempt to drive a wedge into other relevant facets and disciplines. The unanswered questions of atheism soon surface, both in their assumptions and conclusions. Academic attempts have been made to run from these questions, but they have a way of painfully catching up in life's most tender moments and inescapable realities. Conversely, I will argue that the claims of theism are both strong and valid for the mind to espouse and the life to embrace. It is important that we take this many-sided look, because while man may own religion at the level of meaning, he often disavows it at the level of reasoning.

The Assault Begins

Atheism has never lacked a spokesperson. When one considers the impact of even a few of its noted defenders in recent centuries, the handwriting must have been clearly on the wall. There would be many a collision and shipwreck as the academic world approached the uncharted seas of outright atheism. The real threat of Galileo's work to the popular mind-set was not in the subjection of the physical universe to scientific study, nor was it in the abandonment of the Ptolemaic geocentric view. What many jettisoned was the validity of ideas such as prayer and providence in a universe that now had purely mechanistic explanations. The application continued upward. If the world itself presented a mechanical model, must not that apply to man, also? Determinism became a familiar word in philosophy and psychology lexicons. The impact of Galileo's discovery had deep-seated ramifications.

If this were not enough of a challenge to the church, the implications of the Darwinian theory sent shock waves throughout Christendom. The idea that humans evolved by natural selection from the animal world lay the axe at the very root of religious belief. Peripheral ideas held by the church fell like apples from a tree after Galileo. Yet with Darwin the gigantic trunk of theism, which had clung tenaciously to the foundation of God as Creator, was being uprooted. From the earlier blow, the authority of the church was suspect, but there was still a place for God. On the heels of Darwinian Theory, theism itself was under severe attack, and an atheistic mind-set was now a "scientifically supported" reality.

Indeed, it was not fantasy that prompted Karl Marx to consider dedicating his *Das Kapital* to Charles Darwin. He requested Darwin to accept the dedication in the English translation. Darwin declined the offer.[5] That notwithstanding, the correspondence between Marx and Engels shows Marx's exuberance for Darwin's thesis. For Marx himself, religion was the opiate of the people, the sigh of the oppressed, and the only illusory sun that revolved around man, so long as man did not revolve around himself. His rationale behind that dedicatory consideration was that he saw how the Darwinian hypothesis provided the scientific substructure to support his economic infrastructure, on which he could build his man-made utopian superstructure. According to Marx, religion had made room for class division, which could never be allowed, else it would impede the flow of history toward a utopian classless society.

This Marxist belief in turn provided the foundational strength needed by Stalin and gave ideological support for his categorical hatred toward religious people that finally yielded his mass obliteration of millions. Atheism was now alive and well in the political arena. Politics confidently divorced religion, for that which science and economic theory had torn asunder, no sane person dared join together.

The one-two-three punch of the Galileo effect (the loss of confidence in providence), the Darwinian deductions (the loss of a Creator-God), and the Marxist presuppositions (a new economic theory based on atheism) were not the only attacks the church sustained. Freud's analysis of religion further wounded the church's credibility by dragging human sexuality out of the sacred quarters of the marriage bedroom and reducing marriage to nothing more than a substitute for sexual independence (just as work was a substitute for economic independence). As far as Freud was concerned, religion was a public version of a private obsession: some people walked on certain sides of the road, others practiced certain behavior with a compulsive obsession. Religious ritual was just one form of that. Freud desacralized ethics, beliefs, and practices, and grabbed the church by the seat of its pants to throw it over the wall of civilization. He branded the hopes and beliefs of the church as "the future of an illusion," the title of one of his books.

The Undertaker Arrives

With such abusive attacks directed at religious belief coming from so many directions, it was left for someone to cast this creature called theism completely out, and exorcise the world of all such influence. The one who did that with ruthless strength was the German philosopher Friedrich Nietzsche. He delivered so devastating a blow to theistic thinking that the word *orthodox* took on a new concept: it now meant being wrong.

Nietzsche despised religion in general, and Christianity in particular, with unbridled fury. Some of his denunciations were as vilifying as could be imagined. In his *Antichrist*, he said:

> I call Christianity the one great curse, the one enormous and innermost perversion, the one great instinct of revenge, for which no means are too venomous, too underhand, too underground, and too petty.[6]

Nietzsche was the most imaginative and articulate modern spokesman for atheism. He formed a hinge between the nineteenth and twentieth centuries. Living from 1844 to 1900, he philosophically and ideologically swayed the twentieth-century mind, a fact from which there would be few detractors.

In his book *Modern Times*, the historian Paul Johnson referred to Hitler, Stalin, and Mussolini as the three devils of the twentieth century. Interestingly, Nietzschean dogma influenced each of them.

So profound and operative was Nietzsche's philosophy upon Hitler that it provided the conceptual framework for his demagogical onslaught to obliterate the weak and inferior of this world. That being done, Hitler would establish the supremacy of the "superman" in an unobstructed and dominant role.[7] Hitler also personally presented a copy of Nietzsche's works to Benito Mussolini. Nietzsche's influence in the geopolitical chess game of the world, with new "kings," and humanity as "pawns," was far-reaching. He also had a great impact on writers such as Bernard Shaw, D. H. Lawrence, and W. B. Yeats. It is said that after Yeats read Nietzsche, his writings were never the same. Nietzsche's influence upon Sigmund Freud and Carl Jung made great inroads into their powerfully persuasive psychological theories as well. And, of course, his ideology provided much of the verbiage and motivation behind the "God is dead" movement among the liberal theologians that shook the ecclesiastical foundations in the middle of the twentieth century.

Indeed, this son of a Lutheran pastor, and a grandson of Lutheran pastors on both sides of his parentage, was the chief coroner who pronounced God "D.O.A. in the twentieth century." He was a most introspective and passionate individual, who gained widespread acceptance in Europe, except from the English-speaking philosophers. They thought his philosophical imprecision and literary approach did not merit admittance to their close ranks, so they gave him only a grudging acceptance. In recent times, however, the doors of English philosophy have creaked upon their hinges to acknowledge his extraordinary impact. The fact is, Nietzsche stylistically broke the mold, and his blunt portrayals of issues at the highest level of sensitivity in human emotions were impossible to escape. His style of writing, pitched halfway between metaphor and literal statement, was something quite extraordinary. Whatever he said had the flair and power of imagination wedded with reality, transferring the image from his mind onto the mind of the reader with riveting force. Freud several times said of him that he knew himself better than any other human being. That diagnosis has a ring of tragicomedy to it, as Nietzsche spent the last eleven years of his life insane.

One may persuasively debate whether Nietzsche knew himself better than any other, but what seems beyond debate is that he dramatized more than any other writer, with more painful honesty, the logical outworking of atheism. He dragged philosophy away from its tendency to escape the concrete application of its conclusions as it climbed the ladder of abstraction. He compelled the philosopher to pay the full fare of his ticket to atheism and to see where it was going to let him off. Nietzsche wanted to look life squarely in the eye, with no God to obstruct his vision, and the picture he saw was agonizing to his mind. He saw no vast mind behind the framing of this world; he heard no transcending voice giving counsel to this world; he saw no light at the end of the tunnel, and he felt the loneliness of existence in its most desolate form. Just as Jean Paul

> *Nietzsche saw no vast mind behind the framing of this world; he heard no transcending voice giving counsel to this world; he saw no light at the end of the tunnel, and he felt the loneliness of existence in its most desolate form.*

Sartre saw no exit from this random existence, Nietzsche saw no entry from the outside into this hermetically sealed and vacuous life. Man was now left to find his own path, and light whatever lamps he chose.

In a sense, Nietzsche was the first western philosopher to face up fully to man's loss of faith in religion. He put down in black and white what many around him felt to be true, but were unwilling to acknowledge as the logical end of their belief. In pronouncing the death of God, Nietzsche not only stepped right into the eye of the storm, he went further, and admitted that the storm clouds were even more devastating and violent than any of God's undertakers had imagined. The paralyzing darkness that fell was not so much an exterior phenomenon crowding inward but rather an inner blinding that spread outward. It was not just that the philosopher's sling had put out the lights; it was that the disorientation of the mind itself would not know whither to turn for light, and the result was terrifying.

Nietzsche portrayed this intensity in his parable called *The Madman*.

> Have you not heard of that madman who lit a lantern in the bright morning hours, ran to the marketplace and cried incessantly, "I'm looking for God, I'm looking for God!" As many of those who did not believe in God were standing together there, he excited considerable laughter. "Why, did he get lost?" said one. "Did he lose his way like a child?" said another. "Or is he hiding? Is he afraid of us? Has he gone on a voyage? Or emigrated?" Thus they yelled and laughed. The madman sprang into their midst and pierced them with his glances.
>
> "Whither is God?" he cried. "I shall tell you. We have killed him—you and I. All of us are his murderers. But how have we done this? How were we able to drink up the sea? Who gave us the sponge to wipe away the entire horizon? What did we do when we unchained this earth from its sun? Whither is it moving now? Whither are we moving now? Away from all suns? Are we not plunging continually? Backward, sideward, forward, in all directions? Is there any up or down left? Are we not straying as through an infinite nothing? Do we not feel the breath of empty space? Has it not become colder? Is not night and more night coming on all the time? Must not lanterns be lit in the morning? Do we not hear anything yet of the noise of the gravediggers who are burying God? Do we not smell anything yet of God's decomposition? Gods, too, decompose. God is dead. And we have killed him. How shall we, the murderers of all murderers, comfort ourselves? What was holiest and most powerful of all that the world has yet owned has bled to death under our knives. Who will wipe this blood off us? What water is there for us to clean ourselves? What festivals of atonement, what sacred games shall we have to invent? Is not the greatness of this deed too great for us? Must not we ourselves become gods simply to seem worthy of it? There has never been a greater deed; and whoever will be born after us—forsake of this deed, he will be part of a higher history than all history hitherto."
>
> Here the madman fell silent and looked again at his listeners; and they too were silent and stared at him in astonishment. At last he threw his lantern on the ground, and it broke and went out. . . .

It has been related further that on the same day the madman entered divers churches and there sang his "requiem aeternam deo." Led out and called to account, he is said to have replied each time, "What are these churches now if they are not the tombs and sepulchres of God?"[8]

Nietzsche's emotionally charged description is not purely imaginative. He had grabbed reality by the throat, and wrestled with the postmortem grimness of a world that had lost its assumed Creator and Provider. The "myth" of God had been exposed and could no longer carry man into his battles. The illusion that, hitherto, had held such strong sway, was now to be wrapped up in the grave clothes of the buried God. To borrow a Freudian analogy, God had been a kind of consolation to humanity living in the nest, yet upon growing up, man gave him his eviction notice. For centuries he had been the pacifier for the infant years of mankind, but now adulthood had shown him to have been merely imaginary.

Nietzsche was well in touch with the potential consequences of burying God. These morticians of the Absolute could easily make the announcement in the obituary column, but what of the morticians themselves who had now lost their own reason for being?

Had the pronouncers weighed the consequences of the pronouncement? The self-destructive force of this eulogy was equal to the philosophical malady of the Cretan who said "All Cretans are liars." Can you believe him? For man, in stabbing at the heart of God, had in reality, bled himself.

This self-inflicted wound at the dawn of the twentieth century was to bleed uncontrollably as the century wore on. In 1966, the cover of *Time* magazine asked, "Is God Dead?" In 1977, it carried a cover story, "Marx Is Dead." This prompted a college cynic to quip, "God is dead, Marx is dead, and I'm not feeling too well myself!"

That, precisely, was Nietzsche's point: the consequences of the death of God would penetrate every avenue of life, and that thought in and of itself would be unbearable. It could prove to be suicidal, if man did not rise up and take charge. In fact, Nietzsche went on to say, because God had died in the nineteenth century, there would be two direct results in the twentieth century.

First, he prognosticated that the twentieth century would become the bloodiest century in history and, second, that a universal madness would break out. He has been right on both counts. More people have been killed because of ideological differences, and destroyed on the battlefields of geopolitical maneuvering, in the twentieth century than in any other century in history, and by some calculations, more than in the previous nineteen centuries put together.

What is ironic about Nietzsche's statement about universal madness is that, as already stated, with almost symbolic power and in a self-fulfilling prophecy, Nietzsche took the first step and went insane himself. He died in 1900, striking somewhat the same note as the lines from Wordsworth's poem, "Resolution and Independence":

> We Poets in our youth begin in gladness,
> But thereof come in the end despondency and madness.

No matter how loudly Nietzsche shouted about a world of supermen who would find a way to live amidst and beyond these blasted ruins of Christian ethics and moral philosophies, his ideology neither answered nor solved the dilemma of a world without God. He relentlessly pursued "the hygiene of knowledge," arguing for some kind of disinfecting filter for thought, devoid of extrinsic value from any authority outside of ourselves. Its purpose would be to screen out knowledge that is "wrong," and strain in knowledge that is "right"—by Nietzschean definitions. Truth, as a category, he subjected to an embargo; "Truth is fiction," said he. Christian morality he delegitimized. Yet, Nietzsche was never able to produce that "sanitation" desired in knowledge. He really left no such legacy, and, in fact, the despair from which he sought to escape haunted him bitterly. In one of his letters he says, "I feel as though I were a pen, a new pen, being tried out by some superior power on a bit of paper."[9]

Modern philosophers and Christian thinkers have tried hard to warn humanity of the volatility of a world without God. In the platonic dictums and prophetic voices of the Judeo-Christian tradition, there is a well-punctuated recurrence of the great divide between the harmony within a life that lives by the truth, and the discord within a life that shuns the eternal verities. The philosopher G. K. Chesterton said that to believe in the nonexistence of God would be analogous to waking up some morning, looking in the

> *The philosopher G. K. Chesterton said that to believe in the nonexistence of God would be analogous to waking up some morning, looking in the mirror, and seeing nothing.*

mirror, and seeing nothing. With no reflection, no perception, no idea whatsoever of the self, there would be nothing to conform to, and nothing to modify. Thus, the Socratic maxim, "know yourself," would be rendered impossible.

The Darkness Deepens

But with these assumptions life would be so unlivable that there have been voices in philosophy, psychology, and sociology which have, in effect, said that even if there were not a God, we would need to invent one to keep us from eating each other up. This idea hearkens back to the statement made centuries ago about the essence and existence of religions. It was said of early Greece and Rome that all religions were, to the masses, equally true, to the philosophers, equally false, and to the magistrates, equally useful. That term *useful* expressed a "fence function," or boundary, in society. But religion that is based on truth, when reduced merely to a sociological function, will disintegrate through abuse. Time has proven, in an even stronger voice, that pragmatism, which by definition is to do whatever works, in the long run does not work because it is captive to the moment. The foundation of moral action must go deeper and farther than utilitarianism.

Nietzsche's declaration that superior men would triumph in the wake of God's demise has more than been fulfilled in terms of "hygienic knowledge." It has brought as a result murderous demagogues who have wrought inestimable destruction. The last chapter of such beliefs has yet to be written. Any attempt to mitigate the overall effect of this is tantamount to reading cartoons while the headlines spell disaster, or proverbially, to fiddling while Rome burns.

Indeed, Nietzsche's legacy of despair and convoluted sense of superiority have disfigured the lives of troubled souls today. The August 2003 issue of *Reader's Digest* documented one such instance in the story of two teenage boys, Robert and Jim, who killed a married couple, two beloved Dartmouth professors: "The two teens had big plans to escape their small town and lead a glorious life of crime. The first step was to find easy targets and take their money—then silence them."[10] In "The Thrill Killers" the authors recount, "Robert read Nietzsche on his own during high school. What particularly drew him was the German philosopher's exploration of nihilism—the existential notion that God is dead and that no moral values exist. Increasingly the boys parroted each other, their ideas becoming truly bizarre. They concluded that Hitler was 'very cunning' and should be admired. Even in tiny Chelsea [their hometown], population 1,250, their friends and family mostly missed the shadows that were falling over these two lives."[11] Whether or not a philosopher can be legitimately blamed for this atrocious act, one can at least see the logic that provides the impetus for such deductions.

The reality of ideas and their consequences is too serious to trifle with, and mere linguistic surgery will not do. The coats of philosophical paint lavishly put on by the atheistic brush cannot hide the foundational cracks engendered by the storms of life. Any attempt at such a cover-up is the ultimate repression, and the inescapable future of an illusion. The death of God will produce no sanitized supermen to pull us up by our cosmic bootstraps. More likely is the scenario envisioned by the late English journalist Malcolm Muggeridge.

> If God is dead, somebody is going to have to take his place. It will be megalomania or erotomania, the drive for power or the drive for pleasure, the clenched fist or the phallus, Hitler or Hugh Heffner.[12]

Muggeridge's conclusion that either a power-monger or a sex peddler would take the reigns in the place of God is very much in keeping with the disarray of society today. Hitler unleashed on the world one of the most mindless, blood-letting orgies of hatred and sadism—the superman solving the problem by getting rid of what he saw as the inferior. The Heffnerian credo has explicitly degraded the dignity of women, while implicitly asserting pleasure and sensuality to be the supreme pursuit of life.

In Nietzschean terms, the cause—atheism, and the result—violence and hedonism, are as logically connected as the chronological connection between Hitler's announcement of his intent in *Mein Kampf* and the hell ushered in by the Third Reich. The deep tragedy of the hour is that this is neither recognized nor studied by those who proclaim atheism as a benefit to and a victory for the human spirit. Man in a generic sense never takes charge, only self-appointed supermen do, as G. K. Chesterton expressed so well in *The Secret People*:

> The last sad squires ride slowly towards the sea
> And a new people take the land: And still it is not we.

Questions for Study and Discussion

1. The German sociologist Max Weber argued that "man embraces religion at the point of meaning." That is, it is our existential longing for meaning—and the innate knowledge that meaning exists—that prompts us to seek God. Would you agree? What examples have you seen of this in your own life and community?
2. Discuss the impact of Galileo, Darwin, and Freud upon the church. In what ways do they continue to influence disbelief today?
3. The author argues that Nietzsche "dragged philosophy away from its tendency to escape the concrete application of its conclusions as it climbed the ladder of abstraction." How did Nietzsche compel a person "to pay the full fare of his ticket to atheism and to see where it was going to let him off"?

2

Is There Not a Cause?

Science has "explained" nothing; the more we know,
the more fantastic the world becomes, and the pro-
founder the surrounding darkness.

—Aldous Huxley

The story is told of a cynic, sitting under a nut tree, carrying on a rather jesting and gibing monologue with God. His grounds for complaint lay in what he considered to be an obvious failure on the part of God to go by the book on structural design. "Lord," he said, "how is it that you made such a large and sturdy tree to hold such tiny, almost weightless nuts? And yet, you made small, tender plants to hold such large and weighty watermelons!"

As he chuckled away at the folly of such disproportion in God's mindless universe, a nut suddenly fell on his head. After a pause he muttered, "Thank God that wasn't a watermelon!"

In our high-paced, information-inundated society, it is certainly going to take more reasons than a falling nut on a questioning head for many to come to the same conclusion as the man in the story. This reasoning process may not be all bad. The danger of a simple

35

faith is simplistic answers. An informed mind can and ought to bring a proportionate response.

Atheism finds itself with access to enormous data, and it must wade through much material to justify its conclusions. In this pursuit it must cross many hurdles that stand in the way to logical, existential, and pragmatic viability. When it cannot cross those hurdles, it must then be willing to look at the viability of theism, observe how well a theist crosses the same barriers, and study the reasons for his conclusions. In this, and in some of the ensuing chapters, I contend that atheism is unable to cross the major hurdles in its path and ends up making either illicit or ill-fated leaps. In some of these efforts, the resulting damage is far greater than others. But cumulatively, the hurdles are ultimately uncrossable, and this failure has immense implications.

By definition, atheism is the doctrine of belief that there is no God. It is an affirmation of God's nonexistence. This ought not to be confused with agnosticism, which claims not to know. Postulating the nonexistence of God, atheism immediately commits the blunder of an absolute negation, which is self-contradictory. For, to sustain the belief that there is no God, it has to demonstrate infinite knowledge, which is tantamount to saying, "I have infinite knowledge that there is no being in existence with infinite knowledge." Let's not, however, get bogged down in the morass of such pedantic verbal dead ends. Other counter arguments are more important.

The first great hurdle to cross is the question of origins, and the ill-fated monumental leap that some scientists are wont to make from the findings of science to atheism. There is little doubt that the theory of evolution provided a massive thrust for ousting God from the paradigm of origin and existence. Since then, the whole terrain of evolution has been so efficiently mined that the Christian walking on tiptoe through it, is bound, sooner or later, to step on one and be decimated, along with all he has cherished.

The history of interaction between theism and evolutionary theory is filled with vitriolic language and vilifying exchanges between competing worldviews. Often, the antipathy manifested by science against religion is either ill-founded or clearly prejudiced. A landmark illustration of that scorn is Thomas Henry Huxley's well-known response to Archbishop Samuel Wilberforce of Oxford at a meeting of the British Society for the Advancement of Science in 1860:

> If the question is put to me whether I would rather have a miserable ape for a grandfather, or a man highly endowed by nature and possessed of great means of influence, and yet who employs those faculties and that influence for the mere purpose of introducing ridicule into a grave scientific discussion—I unhesitatingly affirm my preference for the ape.

It is said that when the Bishop of Worcester later reported these proceedings to his wife, she replied, "Descended from the apes! My dear, let us hope that it is not true; but if it is, let us pray that it will not be generally known."[1] Unfortunately for the Bishop's wife, the story did become generally known.

Biology or Theology

The real tragedy, however, is the big difference between what is known and what is believed. The progress in microevolutionary processes and the extrapolation into macroevolution, with particular application to origins, is neither scientifically nor metaphysically sound. Yet, strong acerbic language, issuing from a grave antagonism towards things spiritual, has often found its way into scientific journals and into the popular writings of journalists. The instances are too many, and the deductions too seriously implicative, to leave them unaddressed. The straying of physics into metaphysics, making repeated inroads into philosophical and theological application, is like a sword being wielded irresponsibly, unlawfully, and hence, with immense danger. Ultimately, the one wielding the sword cuts off his own head.

Thus, the first mistake atheism makes is the illicit leap through science, from evolution to first causes. It is a leap that is unjustifiable. Thomas Henry Huxley, popularly known as "Darwin's bulldog," introduced a militant mood with his tendentious and denunciating arguments. In reviewing *The Origin of Species* in 1860, he waxed eloquent with transcending glee:

Extinguished theologians lie about the cradle of every science as the strangled snakes beside that of Hercules; and history records that whenever science and orthodoxy have been fairly opposed, the latter has been forced to retire from the lists, bleeding and crushed, if not annihilated. But orthodoxy is the bourbon of the world of thought, it learns not, neither can it forget.[2]

His rhetoric spared nothing, and like a giant mastiff, he chewed Christianity to bits and spewed it out. Huxley's thinking went significantly beyond that of Darwin, as award-winning scientist and writer, Stanley Jaki, has pointed out:

The word "evolution" made its appearance in *The Origin* only in the form "evolved," and only in its sixth edition in 1872. The word became a prophetic counterpoint to that Grand Conclusion into which Darwin inserted (from the second edition on) a reference to the Creator as the One who "originally breathed life with its several powers into a few forms or into one." Yet the whole evolution of Darwinism shows that the last phrase in *The Origin* about the Creator is out of place in what evolutionary philosophy, or evolutionism, has by and large come to be. A telling anticipation of this was the conflict between the last phrase of *The Origin* and the third of the three mottos introducing it. Through that motto, a quotation from Francis Bacon, Darwin warned against the presumption of believing that one could, by contemplating nature, be in possession of final truths, either in divinity or philosophy.[3]

Darwin clearly stated in his autobiography that he was a theist when he wrote *The Origin*. His agnosticism on how life began grew over the years, but he felt it was not within his range to come to such philosophical conclusions. Recognizing himself to be a weak metaphysician, he found himself trapped in a maze, not knowing whether the concept of God in his mind was due to the underlying truthfulness of the idea, or whether it was purely a mechanistic inculcation. Yet he certainly did not have the castigating intentions or hopes that Huxley developed.

Huxley's claim that when science and religion have come into conflict, it has always resulted in the decimation of the latter by the former, is neither true nor fair. If Huxley's allegation were true, and his *fait accompli* attitude were warranted, there would not be such a great number of eminent scientists today who reject the metaphysical leap of Darwinism or post-Darwinian thought, to say nothing of the scientists who are avowedly Christians.[4]

Take, for example, Michael Behe, who in his book *Darwin's Black Box*, shows us the irreducible complexity of the human cell, which biological evolution cannot explain. Darwin argued that a human eye evolved from a simpler one, and yet he set aside the essential question of its origin. Behe not only observes Darwin's avoidance of this question but tackles it by describing the chemical changes that are set in motion to generate sight. From the moment a photon hits the retina to the end result of an imbalance of charge that causes a current to be transmitted down the optic nerve to the

> *Darwin argued that a human eye evolved from a simpler one, and yet he set aside the essential question of its origin.*

brain, resulting in sight, a series of chemical reactions have taken place that in evolution's mechanism would have been impossible. Thus Behe concludes that the irreducible complexity of the human cell reveals that biochemically macroevolution is impossible and Darwinism false.

Contrary to Huxley's view, the leap to atheism actually does more to destroy science than theology. Huxley would have done better to have concentrated on the internecine warfare within the scientific world itself, where scientific theories and beliefs have fallen by the wayside as new finds decimate old ones. The move from Ptolemy to Copernicus to Newton to Einstein, and to the high value placed on Quantum Theory, has massive leaps within it.

Science is neither metaphysical nor monolithic, and honest scientists would study their subject with caution and humility, retaining a judicious agnosticism about the limitations of the scientific understanding of humankind. If they do not, they transgress and make a metaphysical leap, turning science into scientism.

Mary Hesse, in her *Criteria of Truth in Science and Theology*, and Jürgen Habermas, in his *Knowledge and Human Interests*, warn of this. Commenting on the role of science and the restrictions it must observe, Hesse reminds us that the knowledge of science "does not yield truth about the essential nature of things, the significance of its own place in the universe, or how it should conduct its life."[5]

Science is not monolithic, I say, because of the various demarcating disciplines that have to converge if there is to be a unified result. In such a vast terrain the many routes have their own built-in restrictions. The distinct disciplines that are necessary in the study of humankind are so varied and demanding that the scientist ought to have a great deal of respect for the challenge he or she faces. These disciplines incorporate the roles of the cosmologist and astrophysicist, the physicist and physical chemist, the biochemist, the molecular biologist, the cell biologist, the anatomist, the physiologist, and the neurophysiologist. How vast is the area of understanding needed.

For example, a neurophysiologist studies the brain (just one intricate strand of study) with its billion long nerve cells, each of which, on the average, makes contact with 10,000 other cells under the control of chemical messengers. Even the brain of an octopus far exceeds in complexity any human artifact, and the human brain is immensely more complex. Charles Sherrington, in *Man on His Nature*, gave a picturesque description, seeing the brain as

> an enchanted loom where millions of flashing shuttles weave a dissolving pattern, always a meaningful pattern though never an abiding one; a shifting harmony of sub-patterns.[6]

This is the magnitude of information from just one physical organ, thus hardly a pursuit for a hobbyist at play. When one adds the other dimensions of a human being's intricate nature, the task is no longer manageable by the physical scientist alone. Humans also function as social and aesthetic beings. Our unique linguistic capacities, our moral struggles, our religious bent, our yearning for love, and our search for personhood only add to the endeavor at hand. This complexity necessitates that scientific theorizing recognize its own limitations, or the conclusions will be severely warped. The progress in science, and its changing theories, quickly demonstrates that Darwinism and its post-Mendelian forms (involving genetic theory) can hardly afford the pejorative summation of Huxley on theology.[7] Scientific facts have often been discarded with fresh discoveries, old laws have surrendered with the advance of new hypotheses. The divergent views of dissenting voices over the last century have been many, and deep-seated conflicts remain. A brief glimpse of the areas of conflict will serve to justify this caution.

Biology or Physics

The conflicts within science are felt on at least three fronts. The first of these is the absence of a unifying system that pulls together the variegated strands into a homogeneous unit. One of the key struggles here is in having to deal with the problem of determinism; that is, are we the product of blind chance? Although several philosophers have dealt with this question, up to this point none has been able to present a unifying theory that gives a satisfactory answer.

Second, evolution itself has been subjected to several major disagreements within the sciences over at least three main periods. In the early part of the century, the debate focused on whether the offspring inherited a blending of the parental characteristics. The whole issue of inherited variations came into great controversy when Gregor Mendel's work was rediscovered, and many bitter words ensued between the Biometricians (those who measure biological material) and the Mendelians. The animosity engendered turned into personal and vilifying exchanges.

The next conflict, between paleontologists and geneticists, raged in the 1920s. As knowledge of mutations increased, a widespread disenchantment with classic Darwinism came about, resulting in the propounding of a variety of other theories of evolutionary mechanism. If one reads the histories of biology of this time (Nordenskiold, Radl, Singer, and others), they portray the evolutionary theory as an illogical mess.

In the 1960s and 1970s the debate on neutralism and selection gained impetus. Two of the key names involved here were H. J.

Muller and J. B. S. Haldane. R. J. Berry, professor of genetics at University College, London, said:

> The theoretical arguments of Muller and Haldane can in retrospect be seen to be rather naïve. Both men effectively thought of every gene acting independently of its carrier. This is patently not true.[8]

Coming right up to our day, American paleontologists Niles Eldredge and Stephen Jay Gould challenged the prevailing orthodoxy that says our lack of knowledge of the origin of species is the result of gaps in the record. Instead, they say, evolution proceeds by fits and starts, and therefore, the gaps are not gaps, but only rest periods in the process. The deductions that follow from this view have brought about further intense debate.[9]

Not only have there been great differences in terms of process, but the third front on which science faces its most serious struggle is in the even deeper conflict about the various possibilities of origins. For example, Sir Fred Hoyle has argued in his book *The Intelligent Universe* that the idea that life originated by the random shuffling of molecules is "as ridiculous and improbable as the proposition that a tornado blowing through a junkyard may assemble a Boeing 747." He calculated that the likelihood of life beginning in such a way is one in ten to the power of forty thousand. (He illustrates this by examining the chance that two thousand enzyme molecules will be formed simultaneously from their twenty component amino acids on a single specified occasion.)

I find the answer of one contemporary scientist to Fred Hoyle rather fascinating:

> But this is not the correct calculation. The relevant chance is some far simpler self-replicating system, capable of development by natural selection, being formed at any place on earth, and at any time within a period of 100 million years. We cannot calculate this probability, since we know neither the nature of the hypothetical self-replicating system, nor the composition of the "primeval soup" in which it arose. The origin of life was obviously a rare event, but there is not reason to think that it is as extraordinary or unlikely as Hoyle calculated.[10]

Note this response. The opening line says, "This is not a correct calculation." The next statement says, "We cannot calculate this probability . . ." The condemnation of Hoyle is made because of an incalculable probability on the basis of an unknown system. The admission is unblushing. Science just does not have knowledge of the beginnings in the genuine sense of the term. It cannot answer the *how*, much less the *why* of there being something rather than nothing.

Yet, many still insist on taking that blind leap. George C. Simpson stated that evolutionary theory arguably demonstrated that the

> *Science cannot answer the* how, *much less the* why *of there being something rather than nothing.*

whole evolution of life could have ensued, and did so, automatically. Simpson said, "There is no need, at least, to postulate any non-natural or metaphysical intervention in the course of evolution." But as Stanley Jaki argued in response:

> Two remarks may be in order, one scientific and one metaphysical. It *is* the scientific burden of a proponent of automatic evolution to account for the nonautomatic features in man's behavior in general, and for the presumably nonautomatic formulation of theories advocating universal automatism. As for metaphysics, it is indispensable to evolutionary process as in relation to its very start.[11]

From a different angle, Lesslie Newbigin, in his book *Foolishness to the Greeks*, addressed the same thorn in the side of the scientists who hold to automatic evolution, rather than an intelligent first cause. One of their deep-seated struggles is to explain thoughts and conclusions that are based in a brain that is purely mechanical. Can the deductions of such a process be really considered true? Referring to the phenomenon and the epiphenomenon of the brain and its relationship to the mind, Newbigin said this:

[H]owever we may explain our mental states, we know that we have them. I think that I exist. If this idea is only a series of electrical pulses in my brain, the capacity of the brain to produce these pulses must be the result of evolution by natural selection. But since the idea that I can by my will affect the operation of these pulses is an illusion, the existence of this idea can have no effect upon what happens in the world of physical and chemical change. Therefore, it can have no bearing on natural selection. Therefore, the existence of this illusion is an unexplained mystery since it cannot have arisen from natural selection. The "explanation" fails to explain.[12]

I might add that this is one of the key issues Darwin struggled with, and it has serious implications for the behavioral scientist. Atheism has never meaningfully defused these questions that force atheistic worldviews into circular arguments. Indeed, addressing the atheist, biologist George Beadle raised the question, "Whence came the hydrogen?" Beadle added, "Is it any less awe-inspiring to conceive of a universe created of hydrogen with the capacity to evolve into man, than it is to accept the Creation of man as man?"[13]

Beadle's point is well-taken. In pushing back the regressive causes, the atheist is not able to escape the inexplicability of an impersonal first cause, to say nothing of the awe-inspiring capacity of the "raw

> *In pushing back the regressive causes, the atheist is not able to escape the inexplicability of an impersonal first cause, to say nothing of the awe-inspiring capacity of the "raw material" from whence it all "evolved."*

material" from whence it all "evolved." The turning of hydrogen into thinking and purposive beings is scientifically undemonstrated, and philosophically devoid of merit.

This whole area is such an insurmountable problem for the scientist that F. H. C. Crick, whose discovery of the DNA molecule has had such a profound effect on genetics and biological life as we know it, has said, "The ultimate aim of the modern movement in biology is in fact to explain *all* biology in terms of physics and chemistry."[14]

Yet, as we progress, we come to a dead end. Biologists have shown that the discovery of the physical basis for the genetic code has made the answer to the question of origins even more elusive. Even if we were to grant that the genetic code is the result of natural selection, it still needs the "machinery" to translate the code into function, and this translation itself depends upon components that are themselves the products of translation. The possibility of this occurring is so small as to amount to zero probability, bringing about a suggestion from Crick that life in bacteria form may have been transmitted to this planet in a missile from some other part of space. We are back to ground zero. Crick, and others who leave God out of the paradigm, constantly end up with an explanation that fails to explain.

Physics or Metaphysics

The ascending of biological forms into more complex and superior designs also comes into conflict with the Second Law of Thermodynamics in Physics. Thermodynamics is that branch of physical science that is concerned with the interrelationship and interconversion of different forms of energy, and the behavior of systems as they relate to certain basic quantities such as pressure and temperature. Since the origin of the physical universe is intensely connected with this area of science, the Laws of Thermodynamics must be held intact.

The Second Law basically states that heat cannot be transferred from a colder to a hotter body without net changes occurring in other bodies. In an irreversible process, entropy (i.e., heat death) always increases. If the pun may be pardoned, the descent into entropy, or total randomness, really boils down to a move from order to disorder, from the complex to the simple.

Shakespeare presented this idea in the farewell speech of his last play, *The Tempest*, where he has Prospero saying:

> Our revels are now ended. These our actors,
> As I foretold you, were all spirits and
> Are melted into air, into thin air:
> And, like the baseless fabric of this vision,
> The cloud-capp'd towers, the gorgeous palaces,
> The solemn temples, the great globe itself,
> Yes, all which it inherit, shall dissolve
> And, like this insubstantial pageant faded,
> Leave not a rack behind.

From the scientific point of view, the question is, How, in this closed order, do biological systems "swim against the entropic stream"? Or to put it differently, how do biological systems climb the ladder of intricacy and order, while the natural world descends to entropy and disorder?

Scientists have attempted to deal with this conundrum in their studies in dissipative structures, which show that biological organisms maintain their structure at the expense of the system, returning heat to the environment. However, as other scientists point out, this still does not explain nor answer the question of how it was that such highly ordered systems as living organisms could ever have come into existence in a world in which irreversible processes always tend to lead to an increase in entropy and thus, to disorder.

In spite of attempts to arrive at a satisfactory answer to the question raised by the Second Law of Thermodynamics, the perplexities remain. A fundamental law of biology must operate in direct opposition to a fundamental law of physics. Scientists argue that the law for the whole does not apply to all of its parts. (This sleight of hand is fraught with serious problems for those who wish to live by their laws.) One way or the other, it goes back to the "primeval soup" somehow having the awesome capacity within itself to rise above fundamental physical laws. And once again, as Lesslie Newbigin observed, the explanation fails to explain. The answer keeps coming back like a chorus with a mantric resonance to it: *chance.*

French biochemist Jacques Monod said without apology, "Pure chance, absolutely free but blind, is at the very root of the stupendous edifice of evolution."[15] Monod brings his song of harmony out of discord, order out of chaos, to a ringing climax with the words:

> The ancient covenant is in pieces; man at last knows that he is alone in the unfeeling immensity of the universe, out of which he emerged by chance. Neither his destiny, nor his duty have been written down. The kingdom above or the darkness below; it is for him to choose.[16]

A Snake or a Rope

Theoretical physicist John Polkinghorne, a colleague of Stephen Hawking and the former president of Queen's College, Cambridge, is eminently known for his scholarship and brilliance in his field. He has been at the forefront of high energy physics for over thirty years. *Physics Bulletin* described his book *The Quantum World* as one of the best books of the genre. Dr. Polkinghorne does a masterful job of refuting those who think science has done away with a theistic world. He challenged Jacques Monod's conclusion that chance, through a process of random shuffling, brought about our world, and pointed out that the problem is particularly acute in respect to the beginnings of life itself.

Polkinghorne argues against the mindlessness of the position that amino acids just randomly strung themselves together to form the protein chain, and strongly asserts that a tightly-knit and intelligible universe such as ours is not sufficiently explained by a random chance process. The exactness of our universe argues for the anthropic principle, which basically states that the existence and sustenance of man is not brought about by a random universe but is dependent on a universe with a very particular character in its basic laws and circumstances. It is like an acute Copernican revolution, not restoring the earth to the center of the cosmos, but linking the nature of the universe with its potential for the existence of man.

So delicate is the balance, and so tightly knit, wrote Polkinghorne, that scientists have felt particularly uneasy about the delicate balance required by the anthropic principle. To alleviate their anxiety some of them have suggested that there might be a portfolio of many different universes . . . arising from an infinite series of oscillations of one universe, ever expanding and contracting, and each time having its basic structure dissolved in the melting pot of the big crunch, thence, re-emerging in a different form in the subsequent expansion of the big band.

Then Polkinghorne added:

Let us recognize these speculations for what they are. They are not physics, but, in the strictest sense, metaphysics. There is no purely scientific reason to believe in an ensemble of universes. . . .
    A possible explanation of equal intellectual respectability—and to my mind, greater elegance—would be that this one world is the way it is because it is the creation of the will of a Creator who purposes that it should be so.[17]

The conclusion should be clear in our minds. Whether it is Crick's speculation that life could have been shuttled here by a guided missile in bacteria form from another planet, or Monod's exaggeration on chance, Huxley's contention that science has delivered a

---

Huxley's contention that science has delivered a mortal blow to theology is a pipedream.

---

mortal blow to theology is a pipedream. One of the tragic lessons of this century is that experts within certain fields draw upon their knowledge to prove virtually anything they want to prove, all along ignoring a unifying truth that gives fair recognition to other disciplines. It appears that the real problem lies in the fact that Huxley in his contention, and those who live under its fallout, seeing the micro-processes of the trees, have lost sight of the macro-necessities contained in the forest.

An ancient Hindu parable tells of a man, in the dark mists of the night, seeing a shape twisting ominously in the wind and mistaking what was a rope for a snake. The atheistic scientist living with tunnel vision, and under the tyranny of a single idea, in the mist of his laboratory, has blundered in reverse, and mistaken a snake to be a rope. In the Eastern parable, the error lay in perceiving that which was dead to be alive; in atheism the error lies in perceiving that which is alive to be dead. Positing a mindless first cause, the atheist has lost the essence of life.

How well I remember a seminar under Dr. Polkinghorne at Cambridge University. In commenting on the built-in factors within this universe, with particular reference to Quantum Theory, he said, with a grin, "There is no free lunch. Somebody has to pay, and only God has the resources to put in what was needed to get what we've got."

Questions for Study and Discussion

1. Regarding the question of origins, explain "the ill-fated monumental leap that some scientists are wont to make from the findings of science to atheism."
2. Mary Hesse reminds us that the knowledge of science "does not yield truth about the essential nature of things, the significance of its own place in the universe, or how it should conduct its life." What do you think she means by this assertion?
3. The author writes, "Science cannot answer the how, much less the why, of there being something rather than nothing." Would you agree or disagree? Why?
4. Discuss the statement, "The atheist is not able to escape the inexplicability of an impersonal first cause, to say nothing of the awe-inspiring capacity of the 'raw material' from whence it all 'evolved.' "
5. How does evolutionary theory come into conflict with the Second Law of Thermodynamics?

3

VIRTUE IN DISTRESS

The world turns and changes,
But one thing does not change.
In all of my years, one thing does not change,
However you disguise it, this thing does not change:
The perpetual struggle of good and evil.

—T. S. Eliot, "The Rock"

Having abandoned an intelligent first cause of origin, the atheist is faced with a major hurdle in establishing the essential nature of man. In every society, no matter what its cultural underpinnings, there is a code of "oughtness." While the specifics may vary from culture to culture, in each case, those specifics are rooted in a prior set of beliefs as to what ought to be. These, in turn, are related to what they consider to be a person's essential nature and purpose. It is, therefore, inappropriate to say that we cannot challenge one's morality, for the beliefs on which that challenge stands are open to defense or refutation. One common agreement emerges: That wherever one finds an "oughtness," it is always linked together with a believed purpose in life. Purpose and oughtness are inextricably bound, and any effort to sever them

51

meets with individual discord and societal disruption. The result is anarchy.

Consider a watch. Any description of its goodness or badness is bound up with what a watch is supposed to do. The story is an old one, but the point it makes is worthy of repetition. On his way to work every day, a man walked past a clockmaker's store. He would ritualistically stop outside and synchronize his watch with the clock that stood in the window of the clockmaker's shop. Observing this routine, the clockmaker one day struck up a conversation with the man and asked him what kind of work he did. The man timidly confessed that he worked as the timekeeper at the nearby factory and that his malfunctioning watch necessitated daily readjustment. Since it was his job to ring the closing bell every day at 4:00 p.m., he synchronized his watch with the clock every morning to guarantee precision.

The clockmaker, even more embarrassed than the timekeeper, said, "I hate to tell you this, but my clock doesn't work very well either, and I have been adjusting it to the bell that I hear every afternoon from the factory at 4:00 p.m.!"

How does he know the right time when the only recourse is to a poorly functioning watch that is in turn corrected by a faulty clock? What happens to a society that does not know which way to turn to gain an understanding of right and wrong? When confused moral philosophers moralize from uncertain starting points, error compounds itself. A self-caused universe does not communicate morality, a silence underscored by Stephen Crane:

> A man said to the universe:
> "Sir, I exist!"
> "However," replied the universe,
> "The fact has not created in me
> A sense of obligation."[1]

In a naturalistic world, there exists neither a sense of obligation in the universe, nor a demand from it.

The atheist, who by definition subscribes to a purely naturalistic view of our origin and essence, in effect is forced to hold to what is called the Whig theory of history, which asserts that the most advanced moment in time represents the time of highest development. Progress judged this way is not so much logical as it is chronological. With that as a given, the point of present achievement, as signaled by a number of philosophers, sociologists, and psychologists, is that moral absolutes are a thing of the past, and any recognized and endorsed moral theory is anachronistic and vacuous. Nietzsche said it this way:

> When one gives up the Christian faith, one pulls the right to Christian morality out from under one's feet. This morality is by no means self-evident. Christianity is a system, a whole view of things thought out together. By breaking one main concept out of it, the faith in God, one breaks the whole. It stands or falls with faith in God.[2]

He was right. One cannot rescue the beneficial aspects of Christian morality while doing away with Christ. One cannot salvage the Ten Commandments while destroying the authority of the books of Moses. Nietzsche considered the Beatitudes from the Sermon on the Mount to be a damning approach to life, for they emphasize the responsibility of man toward the poor and weak of society. According to Nietzsche, a society driven by such an ethic, in effect, is controlled by the losers.

The present abandonment of a moral law is really quite a unique experiment in civilization. This is not to deny the moral struggles of the past. But those past societies, at least theoretically, espoused a norm for determining what was right and what was wrong, some foundation on which to erect the structures of moral rectitude. In our day, there are no foundations, and we are well on our way to becoming moral eunuchs. Of the twenty-one civilizations that English historian Arnold Toynbee mentioned in his history, ours is the first that does not enjoin a moral law or educate our young in moral instruction.

In another sense, also, this forsaking of a moral law is a unique experiment. Although it is not the first time that atheism has been a formalized system, the accompanying loss of absolutes has never been so blatantly and triumphantly espoused. The Indian sage Sankara was the systematizer and leading voice of his society in his eighth-century commentaries on the Vedas. Though a strict monist having no belief in a personal, relational God, he nevertheless was a strong believer in a moral code, and would have branded our unbelief in a moral law a sign of depravity.[3] Though the founder of Buddhism, Gautama Buddha, taught his beliefs as an atheistic system, he had a strong moral code and would have branded our amoral stance ignorant.

But with the givens of our chance existence in this world, the present posture is at least more consistent. The logic of chance origins has driven our society into rewriting the rules, so that utility has replaced duty, self-expression has unseated authority, and being good has become feeling good. These new rules plunge the moral philosopher

> *Having come loose from our moral moorings in this brave new world, we find ourselves adrift in uncharted seas and have decided to toss away the compass.*

into a veritable vortex of relativizing. All absolutes die the death of a thousand qualifications. Life becomes a pinball game, whose rules, though they be few, are all instrumental and not meaningful in themselves, except as a means to the player's enjoyment.

Having come loose from our moral moorings in this brave new world, we find ourselves adrift in uncharted seas and have decided to toss away the compass. Boston college professor Peter Kreeft, in his *Three Philosophies of Life*, stated it very succinctly:

> Ancient ethics always dealt with three questions. Modern ethics deals with only one, or at the most, two. The three questions are like the three things a fleet of ships is told by its sailing orders. [The metaphor is from C. S. Lewis.] First, the ships must know how to avoid bumping into each other. This is social ethics, and modern as well as ancient ethicists deal with it. Second, they must know how to stay shipshape and avoid sinking. This is individual ethics, virtues and vices, character-building, and we hear very little about this from our modern ethical philosophies. Third, and most important

of all, they must know why the fleet is at sea in the first place . . . I think I know why modern philosophers dare not raise this greatest of questions: because they have no answer to it.[4]

Peter Kreeft appropriately underscored the dissimilarities between the ancient ethicists and their modern—and I would add, post-modern—counterparts. The ancient ethicists probed the specifics, dealing with the *what* and the *how* of ethics in order to arrive at a prescription. Contemporary ethicists question more the *why* and the *if* of ethics in order to write a description.

An Alarming Parable

Leading philosopher and ethicist Alasdair MacIntyre is even more pointed in stating the present malady. In his seminal book *After Virtue: A Study in Moral Theory*, he began with a thought-provoking scenario in his chapter entitled "A Disquieting Sugges-tion." He asked the reader to imagine a world in which the natural sciences, through the blunders of a few, have been instrumental in bringing about a universal catastrophe. The ecological change, resulting in calamitous situations, has provoked crowds into riotous behavior and massive destruction. The lynching of scientists, both verbally and actually, coupled with the destruction of all books dealing with science, has brought the world full circle and left it devoid of all scientific knowledge. On the heels of this, a pseudo-political party has come into power, promising to do away with all teaching on science.

As time goes on, some enlightened individuals seek to revive science somewhat, but they do not have sufficient data to put it all together. Although, once again the verbiage of science resurfaces, no clear-cut definitions for the same words, such as "atomic weight" and "specific gravity," are established. Some half-burnt fragments mention them, but no point of reference is evident.

Like any parable, the details ought not to destroy the main point. MacIntyre pictured an imaginary situation in which a scientific worldview is in jeopardy, and the language itself no longer bears reference to the real facts.

If such a scenario ever became reality, two further complications would arise. First, the logician could not really be of any help, for he would be equally hampered by being locked into the data on hand. He would be able at best to deal only with that which was "known" or "believed." Second, the existentialist, who lives by the force of his will, could call the solutions offered neither right nor wrong, for, in his passion, being quite autonomous, he would choose what he felt to be self-authenticating personally. In such circumstances, would a scientific theory be established on the basis of a popular vote?

Thus, with the foundation destroyed and priority being given to feeling, society would be left with a rugged individualism, each person under his or her own apple tree, determining why he or she feels apples fall to the ground. Having lost the truth base, the "felt," or intuitive, remains an option for all. The sociologist would make his contribution on the basis of a survey, and then scientific norms could be postulated depending on whatever is plausible for most people. Although this would vary from community to community, it ought not to be considered serious because no empirical evidence matters in a salvation-by-survey society. Existence is all that counts. With no fact as a referent, what is normative is purely a matter of preference.

MacIntyre's illustration is very powerful and his application of it very specific:

> The hypothesis which I wish to advance is that in the actual world which we inhabit the language of morality is in the same state of grave disorder as the language of natural science in the imaginary world which I described. What we possess, if this view is true, are the fragments of a conceptual scheme, parts which now lack those contexts from which their significance derived. We possess indeed simulacra [i.e., a vague resemblance] of morality, we continue to use many of the key expressions. But we have—very largely, if not entirely—lost our comprehension, both theoretical and practical, for morality.[5]

MacIntyre's imaginary situation fulfills Nietzsche's parable "The Madman." Between the psychological effect of the incident with

Galileo, the extrapolational leap from the Darwinian theory into atheism, and the philosophical attempt to choke the concept of God by denying it metaphysical breathing room, no logical basis is left for morality. It has been effectively eroded one step at a time. To believe in the defense of morality is considered no longer intellectually tenable.

The Ideas Propagated

One might legitimately ask whether the general public really derives its ethical beliefs from the intellectual pundits of the day, and the answer to that is both yes and no. The pundit of intellectual and debating ability provides ideological and philosophical strength to the institutions of the land, be they legal, educational, religious, or political. The platonic deduction that all politics is law, and all

> *Living under the tremendous illusion that personal freedoms and freedom of speech are devoid of moral assumptions and responsibilities, we have bankrupted ourselves.*

law is ethics, is no longer believed. Living under the tremendous illusion that personal freedoms and freedom of speech are devoid of moral assumptions and responsibilities, we have bankrupted ourselves, so that honor, truth, and morality have been sacrificed at the altar of autonomy and self-worship.

If we are to understand our present moral confusion, we must retrace the footprints that have led to this situation. Without a doubt, the intellectual community must bear the brunt of the blame. Many intellectuals and so-called trendsetters of society have ridiculed the traditional underpinnings of right and wrong and have launched a three-pronged attack upon treasured beliefs: first, by their writings and pronouncements; second, by the changes they have effected upon foundational institutions, such as law and education; and third, by the blatant disregard for morality in their own lifestyles.[6] Thus, institutions that were established to provide the facts for society have now become largely self-serving and provisional. We are left with the fundamental presupposition that right and wrong are ideas without any point of absolute reference. The intellectual supermen have done their job.

As these opinion-makers jumped on the bandwagon of a world now in high gear without God, they held out their philosophical swords to slice up anything in their way. Their proclaimed creed became "knowledge at any price," and this knowledge-for-the-sake-of-knowledge mentality has been categorized as "a lust for knowledge." ("Always learning but never able to acknowledge the truth" [2 Tim. 3:7] is an apt biblical description of such individuals.) These intellectuals have wanted every curtain and veil removed—right down to tinkering with unborn fetuses. All proverbial and parabolic instruction from the past that enjoined reverence and humility has been cast to the winds. The conclusions of the past have been dismissed as primitive belief, and described as a system of thought concocted by a few to control the masses through guilt.

What the intellectual has completely missed is that morality is not abstract or contrived. It is imperative that the historian, the scientist, and the philosopher be in pursuit of what is prescriptively and descriptively true. Further, these findings must be reported truthfully. Philosophy may begin with wonder, but its motivation is the love of wisdom—the knowledge and application of truth. When intellectuals violate morality in any academic discipline, implicitly or explicitly, it leads to lawlessness and the concoctions of science-fiction. And lawless people use their power over nature to control others.

A fierce dog may protect us from the possible ravages of others, but how do we protect ourselves from the intellectual arrogance that plunders everything treasured and leaves it to be mocked and expelled by academicians and celebrities? The heroes of our society win Nobel Prizes or Academy Awards, and then use that platform to castigate moral law. How does the person in the street counter a Nobel laureate or a Hollywood movie star?

Thus, people like Bertrand Russell and Jean Paul Sartre, and even Woody Allen, have had a profound impact on society, having both argued against the existence of God and mocked his injunctions. One would think that such intellectual giants would come up with a compelling argument for their own moral philosophy. Yet, it has not been forthcoming.

Indeed, in his famous debate in 1948 with the philosopher Frederick Copleston, Bertrand Russell revealed his philosophical Achilles' heel on morality. At the midpoint of the debate, Copleston asked Russell on what basis he differentiated between right and wrong, and Russell answered that he did so on the same basis that he differentiated between yellow and blue. Copleston challenged the analogy because colors, he said, were differentiated on the basis of seeing. How does one differentiate between good and bad? And Russell replied that he did so on the basis of his feelings.[7]

Copleston was very gracious, for had he wanted to draw philosophical blood, he could have decimated Russell's argument. In some cultures people love their neighbors, in others they eat them, both on the basis of feeling. Would Russell have had a preference?

Secular philosophers cannot logically give an answer to this question of how to determine right and wrong because there is no common starting point for ethical theorists, and it is not for the lack of trying. Valiant attempts have been made, with some appealing and commendable arguments. But they inevitably reason in a circle and become lost in the maze of counterarguments. Complicating it all are the insatiable passions of humanity, which make an atheistic unifying theory ultimately unreachable.

The English poet and essayist F. W. H. Myers told of the occasion when, on a rainy evening in May, he was strolling in the Fellows' Garden of Trinity College in Cambridge in the company of the great novelist Mary Ann Evans (who wrote under the male pseudonym of George Eliot). They were discussing morality and religion. Myers wrote:

> [S]he, stirred somewhat beyond her wont, and taking as her text the three words which have been used so often as the inspiring trumpet-calls of men—the words *God*, *Immortality*, *Duty*—pronounced, with terrible earnestness, how inconceivable was the *first*, how

unbelievable the *second*, and yet how peremptory and absolute the *third*. Never perhaps, have sterner accents affirmed the sovereignty of impersonal and unrecompensing Law.[8]

It has great appeal to say, "Duty!" But again, if natural selection is a starting point, the questions of duty to whom, and to what purpose, are not answered. An infinite number of theories have emerged to explain "duty," but they keep sliding down slippery slopes.

The theories are well labeled: subjectivism, emotivism, egoism, utilitarianism, and others. Whichever way they move, each system arrives at the edge, or the heart, of autonomy, which literally means a law unto one's self. Jeremy Bentham illustrated in his "greatest happiness principle" the absurd lengths to which philosophers have gone. A pleasure "calculus" was derived to which any action should

We have educated ourselves into imbecility.

be subjected and measured as to duration, intensity, propinquity, extent, certainty, purity, fecundity, etc.

This shows the utterly ridiculous limits to which we have been driven, and it still does not answer the questions of *why* we should be moral and *who* should determine morality. In fact, the extremes to which the human mind has gone in the construction or destruction of moral frameworks well justifies the castigation by Malcolm Muggeridge, albeit cynical, that we have educated ourselves into imbecility. Our philosophers, therefore, however well-intentioned they may have been, have cut the nerve of morality in trying to breathe life into it apart from God.

A Predictable Consequence

Having accomplished the academic slaughtering, these intellectuals separated their mental skills from their moral practices in their own lifestyles, and many who espoused an autonomous morality lived it to its tragic end. The morality of Bertrand Russell, or Jean

Paul Sartre, or Ernest Hemingway betrayed lives lacking cohesion. These authors lived in relationships devoid of love's commitment or moral fidelity. Yet the colossal impact they have had is truly staggering, and their examples ought to give us the courage to recognize the deep and dangerous flaws in the teachings and lifestyles of these molders of the modern and postmodern mind.

Jean Paul Sartre, guru of the sixties, whose name was a household word among students, fanned the existentialist flame of that era. His most enduring mistress, Simone de Beauvoir, said that the slogan from the Sartrean mind-set that enthused her the most was, "It is forbidden to forbid." Through his writings he became the academic godfather to many terrorist movements on the cutting edge of oppression in that decade. Paul Johnson, the historian, said this of Sartre:

> What he did not foresee, and what a wiser man would have foreseen, was that most of the violence to which he gave philosophical encouragement would be inflicted by blacks not on whites, but on other blacks. By helping Fanon to inflame Africa, he contributed to the civil wars and mass murders that have engulfed most of that continent from the mid-sixties onwards to this day. His influence in Southeast Asia, where the Vietnam War was drawing to a close, was even more baneful. The hideous crimes committed in Cambodia from April 1975 onwards, which involved the deaths of between a fifth and a third of the population, were organized by a group of Francophone middle-class intellectuals known as the Angka Leu (The Higher Organization). Of its eight leaders, five were teachers, one a university professor, one a civil servant, and one an economist. All had studied in France in the 1950s where they had not only belonged to the Communist Party, but had absorbed Sartre's doctrines of philosophical activism and "necessary violence." These mass murderers were his ideological children.[9]

The intriguing contradiction in Sartre is that he severely criticized the involvement of the United States in Vietnam as immoral, while he himself walked the logical road from existentialism—which espouses ethical neutrality—to Marxism, from a rugged individualism to a "classless society." A logical road, I say, because I firmly believe that all autonomous cultures over a period of time will need some kind of a mystification and "moral cause." Having rejected God, and finding no cause worthy of total commitment, they move to the utopian ideal of the Marxist worldview, gathering the herd under their "superman wings."

However, Sartre's impact on people of the 1960s is small compared to Nietzsche's influence on Adolf Hitler. Hitler took Nietzsche's writings as his philosophical blueprint and provoked the bloodiest, most unnecessary, most disruptive war in history, changing irremediably the pattern of the world. Nietzsche's influence on Hitler is undeniable. In fact, historian William Shirer has written that "Hitler often visited the Nietzsche museum in Weimar and publicized his veneration for the philosopher by posing for photographs of himself staring in rapture at the bust of the great man."[10]

Probably one of the darkest spots in our world today is what remains of the concentration camp in Auschwitz, in the south of Poland. It was there that Rudolph Hoess, the commandant, oversaw the obliteration of 12,000 people a day. One visit to a place like that is enough to leave one speechless with grief. It reveals the depth of criminality to which the human mind can degenerate. One room contains 14,000 pounds of women's hair, taken from the women after their bodies were removed from the gas chambers, and used for making sacks for transporting commodities. Eugene Kogan's book *Theory and Practice of Hell* described the horror of the Nazi experiment. These were the "new games" invented, to use Nietzschean terminology, on the playing field of the Nazi world. Hitler took Nietzsche's logic and drove the atheistic worldview to its legitimate conclusion. In Auschwitz the words of Hitler are clearly stated:

> I freed Germany from the stupid and degrading fallacies of conscience and morality. . . . We will train young people before whom the world will tremble. I want young people capable of violence—imperious, relentless and cruel.

He took the metaphysic of Darwinian theory, and in his *Mein Kampf* said:

If nature does not wish that weaker individuals should mate with stronger, she wishes even less that a superior race (like the Germanic race) should inter-mingle with an inferior (like the Jewish race). Why? Because, in such a case her efforts, throughout hundreds and thousands of years, to establish an evolutionary higher stage of being, may thus be rendered futile.[11]

What is truly instructive about Hitler's use of natural selection is that Darwin himself foresaw such implications and repercussions from his theory. In commenting about the Civil War in America, Darwin said, "In the long run a million horrid deaths would be amply repaid in the cause of humanity."[12] Elsewhere, he added, "Looking at the world at no distant date, what an endless number of lower races will have been eliminated by the higher civilized races throughout the world."[13]

If atheism gains its life-sustaining support from atheistic evolution, then it cannot shut the floodgates to the tidal waves of its philosophical implications. It is important to keep this in perspective. Augustine warned that it is not wise to judge a philosophy by its abuse. But the theory of the domination of the strong over the weak is not the abuse of natural selection; rather, it is at the heart of it. Hitler unintentionally exposed atheism and dragged it where it was reluctantly, but logically, forced into its consequences. The denuding of people, in every sense of the word, that took place in the concentration camps, brought about the logical outworking of the demise of God and the extermination of moral law.

While Hitler was relentlessly pursuing the "inferior" of the world, leading the most educated nation of the day, Josef Stalin (described by Malcolm Muggeridge as "that murderous Georgian brigand in the Kremlin") began his exterminations of the "inferior" on the uneducated masses. Stalin, who once studied for the priesthood, found moral power to be innocuous compared to brute power. Thus, appointed by Lenin to subjugate beliefs inimical to the revolution, he was selected, among other reasons, because of his hatred for God and for things religious. Now, as Russian historians tally the numbers murdered, estimates have already reached fifteen million people. One historian has said that while Hitler seduced Germany, Stalin raped Russia—both propelled by an atheistic worldview.

Relativized morality, when it has had its day, will have trivialized human beings, and made us expendable statistics in fulfilling the ideological plan of some superman. And if, perchance, one thinks we are too far afield from atheism in our argument, let me remind the reader that it was Nietzsche who said that because God had died in the nineteenth century, the twentieth century would become the bloodiest century in history. Disregard for the sanctity of life, and its resultant corollary of estimating the value of a life by its quality, provided some of the Third Reich's metaphysical moorings. The "inferior" were to be obliterated; the "superior" were to determine destiny, and the will and power of the superman would dominate.

Ironically, at the Nuremberg trials, when the judges on trial were being defended, one of the strongest arguments was that they were operating according to the law of their own land. To that, a legitimate counterquestion was raised, "But is there not a law above our laws?" The Nietzschean answer would have to be "No." Human reason alone, unfounded on a divine first cause, makes survival the only ethic, and it never answers *when*, *why*, or *who*.

It is important that I be clearly understood. Not all atheists are immoral, but morality as goodness cannot be justified with atheistic presuppositions. An atheist may be morally minded, but he just happens to be living better than his belief about what the nature of man warrants. He may have personal moral values, but he cannot have any sense of compelling and universal moral obligation. Moral

> *Not all atheists are immoral, but morality as goodness cannot be justified with atheistic presuppositions.*

duty cannot logically operate without a moral law; and there is no moral law in an amoral world.

Further, just in case it is argued that atheism is not the only philosophy that has resulted in war, and that the Crusaders engendered much violence in the name of Christ, the answer is quite straightforward. Those who, in the name of Christ, have sought to kill in order to propagate their belief, were acting in serious contradiction to both the message and the method of the gospel. By contrast, the demagogues of the Nietzschean and Sartrean stripe were operating in total harmony with, and in some cases the direct injunction of, the ideology behind their actions.

Moreover, we would be deceived if we falsely concluded that the philosophy of atheism has not yet affected *us* with violence. To relegate it to a distant impact would be to assume that the consequences of such ideas, as espoused by these intellectuals, have affected only remote geographical areas or exceptional cases such as the Third Reich. Intellectuals who have eradicated God from their philosophies have not remained content in affecting that remote a sphere. Much closer to home their ideas carry enormous weight in decision-making at the highest levels of our nations, building into the body of society the nerve and sinew of their values in law and education. The filtered-down effect of their beliefs is far-reaching.

The very laws of the land today are shaped by many who have a worldview that denies the moral law of God. We have now found ourselves embroiled in debates that have sweeping consequences, which we try to play on middle ground, living under the illusion of neutrality. As the English philosopher G. K. Chesterton said:

> For under the smooth legal surface of our society, there are already moving, very lawless things. We are always near the breaking point, when we care for only what is legal, and nothing for what is lawful. Unless we have a moral principle about such delicate matters as marriage and murder, the whole world will become a welter of exceptions with no rules. There will be so many hard cases that everything will go soft.[14]

Those words were written more than a generation ago, and now, in that short span of time, the comment by political science professor Robert Fitch has become painfully real:

> Ours is an age where ethics has become obsolete. It is superceded by science, deleted by philosophy and dismissed as emotive by psychology. It is drowned in compassion, evaporates into aesthetics

and retreats before relativism. The usual moral distinctions between good and bad are simply drowned in a maudlin emotion in which we feel more sympathy for the murderer than for the murdered, for the adulterer than for the betrayed, and in which we have actually begun to believe that the real guilty party, the one who somehow caused it all, is the victim, and not the perpetrator of the crime.[15]

Once again, it is key to point out how time has nudged ideas into consequences. The well-known work of Alan Bloom, *The Closing of the American Mind*, was preceded forty years earlier by a book by Richard Weaver (also from the University of Chicago) titled *Ideas Have Consequences*. Weaver's book provided the prophetic backdrop to Bloom's portrait of the closed-minded postmodern skeptic. The impact of ideas has come home in more ways than we realize.

The ideas of atheistic thinkers have shaped this century in a way that few would be willing to deny. *Newsweek* columnist George Will has appropriately said that there is nothing so vulgar left in the human experience for which we cannot fly in some professor from somewhere to justify it. The lesson is obvious: To be an intellectual is a great privilege, but to be an intellectual without God is dangerous. The rock group King Crimson expressed it well years ago when they sang of knowledge being "a deadly friend when no one sets the rules."

An Unworthy Influence

The negative impact upon society has come not only through the arguments of the intellectuals. It has also come more forcibly through their lifestyles and those of the trendsetters, which provides further justification for personalized values. The term *values* is Nietzschean, for morality has no market usage any more. Alan Bloom correctly traced back the word *values* through Max Weber to Nietzsche. The lives of intellectuals often defy explanation; Alexander the Great conquered the world but couldn't overcome his alcoholism.

Paul Johnson, in his noteworthy book *Intellectuals*, raised this issue of lifestyles repeatedly. His chapter titles alone throw into the light the deep-seated, untamed passions of many of those who have shaped society. One of the most heartrending descriptions in the book is in the paragraph that ended his treatment of Jean Paul Sartre, where he drew some very poignant material from Simone de Beauvoir and her book *Adieux: A Farewell to Sartre*. She had become quite disillusioned by his life toward the end and portrayed her years with him in rather brutal terms, describing his unbridled promiscuity, his incontinence, and his drunkenness. His life, like Bertrand Russell's, failed to achieve any coherence. Johnson tellingly ended that chapter (entitled "Jean-Paul Sarte: 'A Little Ball of Fur and Ink' "):

> Over 50,000 people, most of them young, followed his body into Montparnasse Cemetery. To get a better view, some of them climbed into trees. One of them came crashing down onto the coffin itself. To what cause had they come to do honor? What faith, what luminous truth about humanity, were they asserting by their mass presence? We may well ask.[16]

In this brief comment, Johnson summed up one life. The deep reserve we should have about intellectuals of this stripe is climactically stated in the following excerpt from Johnson's last chapter, "The Flight of Reason." Not all will be willing to heed his warning, but a failure to do so will force history to repeat its mistakes.

> One of the principal lessons of our tragic century, which has seen so many millions of innocent lives sacrificed in schemes to improve the lot of humanity, is—beware of intellectuals . . . For intellectuals, far from being highly individualistic and non-conformist people, follow certain regular patterns of behavior. Taken as a group, they are often ultra-conformist within the circles formed by those whose approval they seek and value . . . [enabling] them to create climates of opinion and prevailing orthodoxies, which themselves often generate irrational and destructive courses of action. Above all, we must at all times remember what intellectuals habitually forget: that people matter more than concepts and must come first. The worst of all despotisms is the heartless tyranny of ideas.[17]

In our postmodern context there is no outside value to values. Values depend purely on what one chooses to fuse into them. The intellectual muscle and aberrant lifestyles of many in their sophisticated ranks gave the average man and woman both academic and pragmatic justification to do likewise. These new values, emptied into a milieu that itself had wedded industrialization and urbanization to consumerism and hedonism, have made the whole situation as devoid of morality as any epicurean could have dreamed. Intellectual resources provided the academic capital for many to break away from the Edenic restrictions and expend themselves. When thrown into the bright lights of the city, there was a demand for everything, except morality.

The extent to which this has signaled some calamitous conditions in life and death situations would have been unthought of a generation ago. The universal solvent "the death of God" has effectively dissolved the life-sustaining crucible of morality. But like all universal solvents, the problem of how and where to contain it becomes paramount. Atheistic philosophers cannot provide an answer. Addressing the devastation wrought by the erasing of right and wrong, Shakespeare wrote centuries ago:

> . . . right and wrong
> Between whose endless jar justice resides
> Should lose their names, and so should justice too.
> Then everything includes itself in power,
> Power into will, will into appetite;
> And appetite, an universal wolf,
> So doubly seconded with will and power,
> Must make perforce an universal prey,
> And last eat up himself.[18]

Writing in 1970, Bertrand Russell makes a very revealing statement in the prologue to his autobiography. He said that there were three passions that controlled his life: the longing for love, the search for knowledge, and the unbearable pity for the suffering of mankind. None of these three passions, I might add, could he have truly pursued without a moral imperative.

Philosophers sever the nerve of life if they do not acknowledge a moral law. Having destroyed that possibility by "killing God," they have passionately tried to live out the consequences of their own ideas. And they have ended up like the man in the evolutionary tree drawn in *Newsweek* magazine in 1974—just hanging in space with no support. Morally, they are still trying to build a man out of the tooth of an extinct pig.

Only a moral system that is logical, meaningful, and practical has answers for any society. In hard terms, the morality that atheism teaches, implies, or espouses is unlivable. The dead-end street to which atheism has brought us is appropriately summarized, though

> *In hard terms, the morality that atheism teaches, implies, or espouses is unlivable.*

mildly stated, in a comment by a modern educator. In reply to the question on what positive answers Nietzsche could give to life as it could be lived without God, J. P. Stern, professor of German, University of London, said:

> The answers to that question are, I'm afraid, very unsatisfactory as far as Nietzsche is concerned. His whole attitude towards social questions never does get too far. . . . Nietzsche's recommendations make living together in some kind of harmony extremely difficult. . . . In a sense we can say that some of the more outrageous political doctrines of our time, some of the fascist politics of the early part of this century are based to some extent—among intellectuals, at any rate—on this view that you must create your own values and live by them, regardless of the consequences. It hasn't got us very far, as you can see.[19]

Questions for Study and Discussion

1. Explain Nietzsche's argument that "when one gives up the Christian faith, one pulls the right to Christian morality out from under one's feet." (See full quote p. 53.) Have you

witnessed this appeal to morality by those who argue that such a standard doesn't exist? How might you respond to them?

2. Drawing upon, among others, Alasdair MacIntyre's argument and Nietzsche's parable "The Madman," the author shows that "no logical basis is left for morality. It has been effectively eroded one step at a time." Discuss his conclusion.

3. Consider the assertion that whatever secular philosophy one may ascribe to, "it still does not answer the questions of why we should be moral and who should determine morality."

4. "Not all atheists are immoral," writes the author, "but morality as goodness cannot be justified with atheistic presuppositions. An atheist may be morally minded, but he just happens to be living better than his belief about what the nature of man warrants." What does this tell us about the disconnect between our hearts and our minds? Do you see examples of this disconnect in your own life?

5. Describe how "the morality that atheism teaches, implies, or espouses is unlivable." Would you agree or disagree?

4

SISYPHUS ON A ROLL

Young people are free to conquer the world—and they don't want it. Material prosperity has not made life meaningful. The hunger for love and real meaning are the forces behind the psychedelic revolution.

—Allan Cohen

In 1851, Matthew Arnold penned his poem "Dover Beach." He described the calmness of the sea and the rhythmic flow of the waves moving back and forth. The melancholy it induced in him lifted his thoughts to the tragic turn of the tide in spiritual matters in his English homeland. Once her faith had seemed strong, but that strength had waned, and the calmness was being overwhelmed by a gathering storm of skepticism. The third stanza of his poem expressed this concern on his mind.

> The Sea of Faith
> Was once, too, at the full, and round earth's shore
> Lay like the folds of a bright girdle furl'd.
> But now I only hear
> Its melancholy, long, withdrawing roar,

Retreating to the breath
Of the nightwind, down the vast edges drear
And naked shingles of the world.

Don Cupitt, dean of Emmanuel College, Cambridge, and an
ordained clergyman, took the sentiments of the third stanza of
this poem, particularly the first line of that stanza, and produced
a powerful television series for the BBC, called *The Sea of Faith*.
Cupitt subsequently expanded the material and compiled it into a
book by the same title, making an unblushing and radical attack
upon orthodox Christianity. With the lines from the third stanza of
Arnold's poem as his starting point, he has attempted to drive sharp
wedges into historic Christianity and the classic theistic worldview.
After his eloquent endeavor at "God battering," he had built his own
system of belief, which one critic has aptly called, "faith at sea."

I mention the title and the inspirational role the poem played
in Cupitt's book to point out something that struck me as most
fascinating. There is a rather intriguing omission by Cupitt of the
fourth stanza of Arnold's poem. It does not take very long to understand why that stanza was left out. It runs counter to Cupitt's
central thesis. He is attempting to establish a life with meaning in
a world without God, a possibility Matthew Arnold clearly decried
in the fourth stanza.

Ah, love, let us be true
To one another! for the world, which seems
To lie before us like a land of dreams,
So various, so beautiful, so new,
Hath really neither joy, nor love, nor light,
Nor certitude, nor peace, nor help for pain;
And we are here as on a darkening plain
Swept with confused alarms of struggle and flight,
Where ignorant armies clash by night.

There is no doubt in Arnold's mind (as we know from his other
writings) that with the loss of God came the loss of joy, love, light,
peace, certitude, and help for pain. We are left on a "darkening
plain."

But Cupitt can be forgiven for this volitional blind spot. He is keeping step with others, who, likewise, have sought to do away with God but have refused to deal with the legitimate consequences of meaninglessness. This is where Nietzsche deserves admiration for his candor. He did not play verbal games with abstract arguments, heavily footnoted, to deny the obvious. The great struggle for meaning, encompassed within a deep sense of alienation, is a necessary result of the atheistic worldview. The loss of a creator and the abandonment of a moral law lead to the third hurdle for atheism—the search for meaning. And the lives of millions attest to its failure.

Those who came through the 1960s will remember the spate of conferences at that time with the theme "Who Am I?" It seems

> *The loss of a creator and the abandonment of a moral law lead to the third hurdle for atheism— the search for meaning.*

rather anomalous that dogs and cats never wonder about what dogginess or cattishness entails. We humans are the only ones who raise this question, and we are supposed to be the most informed of the species.

The sarcasm of this thought notwithstanding, it is true that many of our miseries are really a reflection of our grandeur. Human beings are incurable questioners, and no matter how many of our peripheral questions are answered, unless the most fundamental of all questions is answered, we sense nothing between ourselves and the great void but our search, which gradually becomes an end in itself.

At one of my lectures on "Man's Search for Meaning," a student rose to his feet and shouted, "Ah, everything in life is meaningless." I insisted that he could not possibly believe that. With an equally intense retort he countered that he did. This repetitive exchange went back and forth a few times. Then, not wanting to exacerbate the young man's frustration and having planned for a safe departure from the campus, I decided to bring the discussion to an end. I asked him if he thought his statement was a meaningful one. There was an acute silence, and then he hesitantly answered, "Yes." I only had to add that if his assertion was meaningful, then everything in life was not meaningless. If, on the other hand, everything was indeed meaningless, his assertion was meaningless too, and, therefore, in effect, he had said nothing.

At the risk of being simplistic, and also being keenly aware of what he was trying to say, the exchange nevertheless demonstrated the inescapability of our malady to meaningfully express our meaninglessness.

It is a most striking feature of the biblical narrative that the man who most thoroughly and unequivocally poured out his heart and mind on the pointlessness of existence was one who knew more, had more, and was renowned more than anyone else in his time—Solomon. His opening lines in the book of Ecclesiastes—"Vanity of vanities! All is vanity!" or, "Meaningless, meaningless! All is meaningless!"—are very familiar, but some have not followed his thinking to the end of the book. Solomon stated this observation about life out of both study and personal experience, and his sense of emptiness is a recurring theme. He described every pursuit he had taken—his range of accomplishment in wisdom, pleasure, work, material gain, and much else. But in the philosophical equivalent of a midlife crisis, he summed it up in these words in Ecclesiastes 2:10–11:

> I denied myself nothing my eyes desired;
>   I refused my heart no pleasure.
> My heart took delight in all my work,
>   and this was the reward for all my labor.
> Yet, when I surveyed all that my hands had done
>   and what I had toiled to achieve,
> everything was meaningless, a chasing after the wind;
>   nothing was gained under the sun.

Having tried everything that his mind could grasp and his wealth could afford, Solomon found that there was a monotony, a circularity, and a fatality to all human endeavor.

The Humdrum of Monotony

He is not the only one, of course, to have echoed this feeling of being disjointed from life's ultimate purpose. One of the most popular stories from Greek mythology is the myth of Sisyphus. Sisyphus was condemned by the gods for having betrayed the celestial ranks by revealing divine secrets to mortals. They sentenced him to roll a massive stone to the top of a hill, watch it roll down again, and repeat the exercise endlessly. His hell was in having to execute a pointless act from which nothing ever came, except a vain repetition that compounded the emptiness. Not by one step, nor by a thousand, nor by ten thousand, was he able to expiate the sin against the gods that brought on this cursed fate. He could do nothing to rescue himself from futility. As a modern rhyme put it:

> A cheerful old bear at the zoo
> He never lacked nothing to do.
> When it bored him, you know,
> to walk to and fro,
> He reversed it and walked fro and to.

Poor Sisyphus couldn't even reverse it for a temporary relief. All kinds of intriguing suggestions have been made, ranging from changing his internal outlook ("If only Sisyphus could have changed on the inside so that he enjoyed rolling stones") to altering his external viewpoint ("If he rolled up a different stone each time, a beautiful building could be built"). Most of humanity understands Sisyphus's plight and has felt his struggle. The repetition of a single act, or the indulgence in a diversity of acts, has not spared humanity from a sense of monotony. We do not have to read Greek mythology or be cynical to come to this conclusion. The condition is universal and cuts across cultures and age barriers. Even children repeat the theme in nursery rhymes:

> The grand old Duke of York,
> He had ten thousand men,
> He marched them up to the top of the hill
> And he marched them down again.

> And when they were up they were up,
> And when they were down they were down,
> And when they were only half way up
> They were neither up nor down.

If it were not for the melody of this rhyme, its informational quotient would not exactly stir the intellect. But neither would Sisyphus's activity. The vain repetition in both instances could produce a sense of futility in even the least of minds.

Solomon's struggle takes us one step further than Sisyphus's plight. He communicated a deeper concept with great pathos, couched in a more reflective mood. Even he, a man who boasted capacities of intellect and imagination that made him the envy of many, and who presided over the most pompous court of his time, was not spared from a sense of futility. Diversity of activity and the unlimited resources at his disposal still brought the inevitable monotony to weary even the best of minds.

This larger point is sorely missed by those philosophers who try to build an escape hatch for the skeptic by saying that it is meaningless to ask the questions of life's meaning. All through the centuries,

> *This larger point is sorely missed by those philosophers who try to build an escape hatch for the skeptic by saying that it is meaningless to ask the questions of life's meaning.*

man has continued to stab away at the question, and its implications cannot be eluded. Aristotle attempted to deal with this question by looking to man's nature. Jean Jacques Rousseau said that our predicament was the result of the artificial passions that were produced by the emotional changes within us as we moved away from nature. There are myriad options offered as a diagnosis.

Lord Byron, who lived and died tumultuously, embodied the spirit of a world with no values. He summed up his life in the second

stanza of a brief poem, written on his thirty-sixth birthday, three
months before his death.

> My days are in the yellow leaf,
> The flowers and fruits of love are gone,
> The worm, the canker and the grief
> Are mine alone!

This problem of meaninglessness, being as intensive and pervasive
as it is, has drawn even the best of philosophers into the bidding
process. It has pulled together some of the most impassioned and
relevant philosophical argumentation. Hence, it is not, of course,
possible within the confines of this treatment to consider every
school of thought represented. But the most commonly held and
defended view shall be subjected to scrutiny.

The previously stated idea—that of changing Sisyphus's attitude
toward rolling stones—does not warrant too great a response at
this juncture, for it completely misses the point of the question,
which has two essential strands to it. First, if naturalism is all that
we have, does not life itself become a mockery of fate and open to
any interpretation, including that of meaninglessness? Why, then, try
to disavow it as a legitimate expression? If there is no God, it is as
valid, if not more valid, than any other provisional conclusion.

Second, this approach of changing his attitude does not really
mitigate Sisyphus's malady, with its haunting perception of aim-
lessness. It does not put "dislocated" man back into place, it only
induces a stupor to kill the pain. Is it any wonder that different
stupefying theories have been attempted, each one only intensify-
ing the problem? The monotony and pointlessness of life remain,
no matter how we try to ignore them. The most articulate spokes-
persons on this futility are artists and poets themselves. As Joni
Mitchell sang, "We're captives on a carousel of time."

Sisyphus and Solomon came to the same deduction, born out
of their experience: monotony finds no relief in adding variety or
changing our attitude about it. Activity does not create meaning;
it is the other way around. If life in its existential expression has
no meaning, then a change of attitude does not change the reality of meaninglessness. It only changes how one functions in a

meaningless world, which was precisely Jean Paul Sartre's point in his book *No Exit*. What difference does it make, when the boat is going down, if one stands on the deck and salutes or plays a last game of poker?

Yet Solomon and Sisyphus are demanding more than momentary enjoyment, or something to tranquilize their boredom. They are not asking for meaning by truncating reality, but they are seeking for an undergirding conviction that can carry them through their existence, giving overall meaning to their lives.

An Answer That Fails

The most effective philosophical argument against the question of meaning is to question the validity of the question itself. Some contend that to raise the question of meaning devalues life. Kurt Baier, a representative of this school of thought, argued that science invariably takes a cause-and-effect view of life, and that, in the view of the naturalist, purpose and meaning are invalid terms. So far, his position is acceptable, but it soon becomes evident that these terms are unacceptable not only because they are out of the range of science, but also because the naturalist does not know what to do with them. Thus, he brands them unnecessary. Baier stated that to ask a person for the meaning or purpose of his life is to diminish the value of the person by reducing his dignity to the level of a means, rather than an end in itself.

This argument has a built-in contradiction. How can one contend that something is devalued unless he knows the real value? How can one know something is counterfeit unless he also knows what is authentic? This approach is caught in a bind, as it constantly uses the words *purposeful* and *meaningful* to argue against purpose and meaning as needful in the human experience. Baier's argument is self-defeating. It is a valiant attempt to give individual efforts of human beings value in themselves, while at the same time robbing individuals of any value in their origin and destiny. What it really suggests is that life has tiny little purposes, but no ultimate purpose. It destroys ultimate value and substitutes something artificial.

There is something very pivotal here. This is a fascinating reversal of the way the naturalist dealt with the problem as it related to the Second Law of Thermodynamics. We recall that in the scientific struggle with the problem of origins, the Second Law was disregarded by arguing for biological progression in the opposite direction to the laws of physics. The physical law states that things move from order to disorder, but evolution moves from disorder to order. The scientist's response was that what applied to the whole did not apply to its parts, so that biological evolution in its parts could swim against the entropic stream as a whole. Now, on the issue of meaning, the naturalist says that what applies to the parts (rolling stones, building temples, etc.) is meaningful, but does not apply to life as a whole. Life is punctuated with tiny little purposes and no ultimate purpose: tiny little values, but no ultimate value.

The seriousness of the naturalists' predicament is that they frequently handcuff themselves with ideas that are mutually exclusive. Their assumptions keep changing, depending on the arena of controversy; hence, the conclusions collide. The rapist rapes because he sees his victim as only a means to an end, having no ultimate value or meaning in herself. The same applies to the criminal act of murder; the murderer does not see his victim as one having value and dignity, but rather, as an object to be removed for his own purposes. Thus, the question of essential meaning and purpose in life, far from reducing the value of an individual, is indispensable to dignity, and not a denial of it. But what else can naturalists do? In attempting to reason their way through the problem, they have become unreasonable; in trying to defuse the question, they blow up the questioner.

Great thinkers have repeatedly warned over the centuries that a departure from God denudes humans and results in the death of meaning. The denial of God and the death of meaning cannot be severed from each other, though interspersed with all the learning, education, and hyperactivity of postmodern human beings. The farther we move from God, the more we devalue man. The Nobel Prize–winning T. S. Eliot summed it up in a powerful way:

> Where is the life we have lost in living?
> Where is the wisdom we have lost in knowledge?

Where is the knowledge we have lost in information?
The cycles of Heaven in twenty centuries
Bring us farther from God and nearer to the Dust.[1]

G. K. Chesterton warned that the insane man is not just one who has lost his reason; he may be one who has lost everything

> *The farther we move from God, the more we devalue man.*

but his reason, because there is more to life than mathematical equations. C. S. Lewis would have called such a one "a man without a chest," a person with no heart. The delights of love, the loveliness of a baby, the wonder of a mother nursing a child, the exquisite strains of majestic music—all these transcend reason yet have real meaning in our lives. What meaning do they have if life itself is meaningless? That must be answered. It is the need for an answer within an individual mind that pleadingly raises the question.

The Question Intensifies

We must not underestimate the search for meaning. There is no shortage of illustrations to demonstrate the deep distress in the mind of a serious questioner. It is very important to follow the argument here, as expressed by the French philosopher Voltaire, because it will help us to put the finger on the nerve of the issue:

> I am a puny part of a great whole. Yes. But all sentient things, born of the same law, suffer like me, and like me, also die.
>   The vulture fastens on his timid prey, and stabs with bloody beak the quivering limbs. All's well, it seems, for it. But in a while an eagle tears the vulture into shreds. The eagle is transfixed by shafts of man. The man, prone in the dust of battlefields, mingling his blood with dying fellow man, becomes in turn the food of ravenous birds. Thus the whole world in every member groans. All born for torment and

for mutual death. And o'er this ghastly chaos you would say the ills of each make up the good of all.

What blessedness! And as with quaking voice mortal and pitiful ye cry, "All's well." The universe belies you, and your heart refutes a hundred times your mind's conceit. What is the verdict of the vastest mind? Silence. The book of fate is closed to us. Man is a stranger to his own research. He knows not whence he comes, nor whither he goes. Tormented atoms in a bed of mud, devoured by death, a mockery of fate.

Voltaire's lament is only one step removed from Solomon's. While Solomon underscored the futility of effort, whether in pleasure or work, Voltaire finds that futility in existence itself; for Death, that archenemy, in a circuitous pattern, destroys each destroyer. Thus, the miseries of each are supposed to make up the good of all, a boomerang of pain and savagery that returns as natural selection.

This is the ultimate good news / bad news joke. The bad news is that there is a war on. The good news is that the undertakers need the business. Voltaire is engaged, with unsparing effort, in a titanic battle between optimism and pessimism. The best known of all his books, certainly one of his finest efforts, is *Candide*. It is the story of a man who, though pummeled and slapped in every direction by fate, tries desperately to cling to his optimism.

As Candide journeys through life looking for happiness, he meets disappointment after disappointment, and his melancholy grows. Seeing a lighthearted Theatine monk in the market square, walking arm in arm with an apparently carefree young woman, he is convinced his search is ended. He makes a wager with his friend Martin that these, indeed, have found the happiness that had eluded him.

Martin willingly takes the bet because of his confidence that unhappiness is central to every life, without exception. (This part in the book is significant and indicative of how Voltaire viewed the church of his day—hypocritical and bankrupt, much concerned with outward regalia, but with little heartfelt concern for meeting the needs of the people.)

As the question of personal happiness is posed to the woman, the myth is very quickly dispelled.

I am forced to continue that abominable trade which seems so pleas-
ant to you men, but which is nothing but an abyss of misery for us.
I came to Venice to practice my profession. Oh Sir, if you could only
imagine what it is like to be forced to caress without discrimination
an old merchant, a lawyer, a monk, a gondolier or a priest, to be
exposed to every kind of insult and abuse, to be often reduced to
borrowing a skirt for some disgusting man to tear off, to be robbed
by one man of what you've earned with another, to be blackmailed
by magistrates, and to have nothing to look forward to except an
atrocious old age, the workhouse, and the garbage dump, you'd conclude that I am one of the most wretched creatures of the world.

Surprised and disappointed, Candide looks expectantly at the
monk, hoping that *his* response would serve as a counterpoint.
Candide observes,

Father, you seem to be leading a life that anyone would envy: you're
obviously in the pink of health, your face is aglow with happiness
. . . and you appear to be quite content with your lot as a Theatine
monk.[2]

But the priest pours his heart out, admitting to a deathly loneliness in the monastery, and to the sheer hypocrisy that is both in
him and around him. As he unfolds his tale of woe and wretch-
edness, Candide, in anguish, knows he has lost his bet. The two
opposite symbols of society—the harlot, a dispenser of pleasure
with no compunction and moral law to bind, and the monk, the
recluse, supposedly celebrating the nobility in man—are equally
wretched. One sees life as a dance, and the other as a dirge, but
both find life to be empty. As Sartre suggested, the poker game
or the salute makes no difference; the boat is still going down.
Voltaire perceived what he did because with every fiber of his
being he was seeking without success the answer to life's ultimate
riddle—the seeming futility of it all. Candide gives us the key
to Voltaire's conclusion of meaninglessness, the same key that
unlocks what Solomon said centuries earlier about pleasure and
religion.

The Problem of Pleasure

To understand what they are saying is pivotal to finding the solution. There is a fundamental flaw in the argument of many philosophers and popular thinkers who argue that the presence of evil brings about the struggle for meaning. On the face of it, the argument sounds powerful, but it brings so much emotional baggage with it that the whole argument gets wrongheaded. The presence of pain and evil in their multifarious manifestations dents even the most robust argument attempting to square life with the purpose of love. One can ignore the problem of evil only by committing intellectual suicide. The problem of evil, however, is not the primary issue in considering the loss of meaning.

For the atheist, there are issues more fundamental than the problem of evil, which forcibly raise the question of life's meaning. For, the fact is, life has been found to be more meaningful for many who are in pain, than for many in pleasure. Prior to the problem of pain is the frustration of meaninglessness even when every comfort we pursue comes within reach. This agony is captured well in the words of Methodist minister and scholar Paul Hoon:

Technology has freed him from the confines of space to travel at 25,000 miles an hour.

Industrialization frees him to move to a new job or a new home, or from a lower to a higher income tax bracket.

Electronics frees him to turn a dial and enter into a multitude of experiences quite foreign to his own. Education frees his mind and his conscience.

Medicine frees him from disease. Psychiatry and chemistry free his emotions.

Music and art free his imagination.

Government, at least in theory, frees him from political decision.

A thousand tyrannies, both inward and outward, have been broken, yet, he is rightly called "homo perturbatus," restless man, intoxicated with such freedom as he has never known before.

For all his gains, the man who travels at 25,000 miles an hour has a nervous breakdown. Affluence and poverty, each in its own way, lock him in.

Television captures his sensitivities and homogenizes his tastes.

Education becomes a treadmill.

Vogues in art fasten upon the public consciousness, and 3 million people buy the same novel.

Drugs enslave.

Wars become stalemated.

Diplomatic negotiations become deadlocked.

The "system," or "establishment," constricts. Anarchy erupts and law answers with (what becomes branded as) repression.

"Determinism" is still a reality term in a psychologist's lexicon, and death still lies at the end of life.[3]

It is easy to understand why apathy, fear, or emptiness is normative, and that each, in its own way, locks us in. Paul Hoon has underscored the real problem and pointed in the right direction. With all of our access to everything that is supposed to make life easier and more satisfying, humans, intoxicated with the abundance of options, find some chains unbreakable.

It is not surprising that *boredom* is a very modern word, with no counterpart in the ancient or medieval languages.[4] Kurt Baier can write any form of argument to repudiate the pursuit of meaning, but human beings will return to it in every generation because of the nature of the malady.

G. K. Chesterton summarized this malady in one epigram—"Despair does not lie in being weary of suffering, but in being weary of joy."[5] I would change just one word in that statement, so that it would reflect our present word usage more accurately—"Despair does not lie in being weary of suffering, but in being weary of pleasure."

This conclusion is not, in any way, to cast a negative connotation upon the word *pleasure*. It can properly describe a legitimate fulfillment, such as the sensation of winning a thrilling tennis match at the Wimbledon Finals, or the imprudent high of a drug addict. The word itself is not to be impugned, for the context determines the interpretation.

To translate Chesterton's idea, then, despair comes not from being weary of suffering, but from being weary of pleasure. When the pleasure button is repeatedly pressed and can no longer deliver or sustain, the emptiness that results is terrifying. Surely, the

loneliest moment in life is when you have just experienced what
you thought would deliver the ultimate, and it has let you down.
Several have expressed this, either in its impassioned form or in an
honest confession of the pursuit of meaning.

Samuel Taylor Coleridge, one of the founders of the Romantic
movement in literature, is renowned for his poetic genius, being
perhaps best known for his poems "The Rime of the Ancient Mari-
ner," "Kubla Khan," and "Christabel." He justifiably argued that

> *The loneliest moment in life is when you have just*
> *experienced what you thought would deliver the*
> *ultimate, and it has let you down.*

the mind has immense creative powers and its use is not a mere
mechanistic process. Yet, at a very significant juncture of his life,
he wrote in his notebook:

> Tomorrow my birthday, 31 years of age—O me! My very heart
> dies . . . Why have I not an unencumbered heart? These beloved
> books still before me, this noble room, the very center to which a
> whole world of beauty converges, the deep reservoir into which all
> these streams and currents of lovely forms flow—my own mind so
> populous, so active, so full of noble schemes, so capable of realizing
> them . . . O wherefore, am I not happy?[6]

As fertile a mind as he had, he knew an emptiness that led him
into opium addiction. Poet William Hazlitt described Coleridge as
one who had swallowed doses of oblivion.

Success and creative strength do not bring meaning to life, even
if they are fulfilled to capacity. The recognition of this was the
very point that led to the conversion of Dr. James Simpson, who
was the discoverer of chloroform. As a surgeon, he had witnessed
painful surgical procedures that sent patients into sheer delirium.
This launched him into a search for an anesthetic, and when he
discovered chloroform, he gave humanity a gift of enormous pro-
portion. In fact, so grateful was his first patient when she gave birth

to her baby under Dr. Simpson's administration, that she called her daughter Anesthesia.

One would have thought that living with and being surrounded by all kinds of pain, he would have been driven to existential despair. Or, conversely, that he would have considered the alleviation of physical pain his greatest discovery. Yet, it was not that which contributed to his spiritual struggle or triumph; rather,

> when benevolence shall have run its course, when there shall be no sick to heal, no disease to cure, when all I have been engaged about comes to a dead stop—WHAT is to fill this heart and thought and power of mine?[7]

A life consumed with benevolence and philanthropy had left his heart unfulfilled. Ironically, this question of his purposelessness was put to Simpson by a woman while she was an invalid under his care. And therein lies the crux of the problem—an invalid, challenging the discoverer of chloroform to seek out the true meaning of life.

I believe this deep struggle is well addressed, though in a subtle form, in the film *Chariots of Fire*. It portrays the great runner, Harold Abrams, as strong, motivated, cocky, intimidating, and self-confident. Asked by a friend in the early part of the story how he felt about losing, Abrams snapped back, "I don't know. I've never lost." Toward the end of the film and moments before his most important race, Abrams looked into the face of the same friend and said, "I used to be afraid to lose, now I'm afraid to win. I have 10 seconds to prove the reason for my existence, and even then, I'm not sure I will."

The point is powerfully reinforced by his dispirited response on the heels of a gold medal victory at Paris in 1924. He had won, but the reason for his existence was no clearer.

Here, then, is the first clue to solving the dilemma of meaninglessness. Even life's pleasures bring the feeling of pointlessness; they are here for a moment and then gone. At best they have "liftoff" power, but no "staying" power, or, to use a different analogy, they are like periodic flashes of lightning on a dark road, with no guiding power.

The Key That Unlocks

But there is a second clue, and it is at the heart of naturalism, defining both its predicament and poverty. Solomon gave us the key to unlock it. In his dead-end pursuits, he repeatedly used the phrase, "under the sun," which denoted life outside of God, viewed horizontally, in a closed system. Voltaire showed us his closed system when he said, "What is the verdict of the vastest mind? Silence." At this point Voltaire and Solomon part company, for Voltaire, in shutting out the vastest mind, remained in his misery, whereas Solomon, by allowing the vastest mind to speak, moved from meaninglessness to meaning.

The Christian contention is that God *has* spoken, and until he has his rightful place in our lives, neither the squandered, immoral life of a harlot, nor the rigorous, self-motivated, ritualistic life of a recluse will have purpose and meaning. The words of Saint Augustine of Hippo (354–430) are most appropriate: "You have made us for yourself and our hearts are restless until they find their rest in Thee." Or, as French mathematician and philosopher Blaise Pascal was known to have put it, "There is a god-shaped vacuum in the heart of every man, and only God can fill it."

Atheism walks with its head down, earthbound, which is why it grasps nothing of eternal value. It must admit its predicament: without God, there is no meaning to life.

Questions for Study and Discussion

1. On pages 73–74 we read about a lively exchange the author had with a student regarding the question of meaning. What leads the author to conclude, "The exchange . . . demonstrated the inescapability of our malady to meaningfully express our meaninglessness"?
2. Regarding the problem of meaninglessness, Sisyphus and Solomon arrive at the same place: "If life in its existential expression has no meaning, then a change of attitude does not change the reality of meaninglessness. It only changes how one functions in a meaningless world." Discuss their conclusion.

How have you wrestled with this search for meaning in your own life?

3. Explain what the author means when he says that the naturalist approaches the two questions of origins and meaning from conflicting starting points, or "with ideas that are mutually exclusive." (See pages 78–79.)

4. Comment on the statement, "There is a fundamental flaw in the argument of many philosophers and popular thinkers who argue that the presence of evil brings about the struggle for meaning." Have you encountered—or made—this argument as well?

5. G. K. Chesterton said, "Despair does not lie in being weary of suffering, but in being weary of joy (or pleasure)." Would you agree? What evidence have you seen of this in your own life and community?

5

GRAVE DOUBTS

Though you forget the way to the Temple,
There is one who remembers the way to your door;
Life you may evade, but Death you shall not,
You shall not deny the Stranger.

—T. S. Eliot

To be, or not to be—that is the question;
. . . To die, to sleep;
To sleep, perchance to dream. Ay, there's the rub;
For in that sleep of death what dreams may come,
When we have shuffled off this mortal coil,
Must give us pause.

—William Shakespeare, *Hamlet*

The subject of death has been addressed by a majority of the great thinkers because it is the last "enemy" and the one common experience we are all forced to face. It is the great human equalizer. But it is also the one subject that is still shelved in the category of "the Unknown," or relegated to a topic that is taboo in polite conversation—the intruder upon happy conversations.

The existential philosopher Albert Camus (1913–1960) said that death is philosophy's only problem. Quite a significant problem, I might add. In spite of all our great learning, this remains the one area where skepticism and agnosticism abound.

In the arena of birth we have somewhat lifted the veil, and have even registered the sounds and impulses to which the baby responds while still in her mother's womb. In the realm of sickness and disease, while new maladies seem to lift their sinister heads and keep the researchers busy, great strides have been made to find cures for many others. The frontiers of knowledge continue to expand with such rapidity that we live with accomplishments undreamed of a generation ago.

Many new vistas have been opened, but the real and felt blindness about death is total. It is the one subject that, according to Aldous Huxley, we have not succeeded in vulgarizing. What is it about death that casts this haunting spell, and has handcuffed the most "civilized" of our societies?

Here, atheism meets its nemesis. Any system that does not know the origin of human beings and cannot give our reason for being, certainly must remain silent on our destiny, or at best, argue for nothingness. American psychologist and philosopher William James said, "Our civilization is founded on the shambles, and every individual existence goes out in a lonely spasm of helpless agony."[1] Apart from the bid for suicide, which is an expression of unmitigated hopelessness and abandonment, the reluctance to face death is quite universal. It is the one experience when we leave behind everything we have and take with us everything we are. It is the moment of truth, where there is no more showmanship. It is the individual alone against destiny.

The actor/director Woody Allen said of death, "It's not that I'm afraid to die, I just don't want to be there when it happens." If he is, indeed, as fearless about it as he claims, the good news for Allen is that he will die, but the bad news is that he will have to be there. When all is said, is it not this aloneness and inevitability that makes the event more dreadful? In death, atheism can offer no comfort whatsoever, and as in the question of our origin, leaves one in the state of an unthinking atom—out of flux, nothing but flux.

Bertrand Russell, without apology, stated the atheistic viewpoint on death:

Such, in outline, but even more purposeless, more void of meaning, is the world which Science presents for our belief. Amid such a world, if anywhere, our ideals henceforward must find a home. That Man is the product of causes which had no prevision of the end they were achieving; that his origin, his growth, his hopes and fears, his loves and his beliefs, are but the outcome of accidental collocations of atoms; that no fire, no heroism, no intensity of thought and feeling, can preserve an individual life beyond the grave; that all the labours of the ages, all the devotion, all the inspiration, all the noonday brightness of human genius, are destined to extinction in the vast death of the solar system, and that the whole temple of Man's achievement must inevitably be buried beneath the debris of a universe in ruins—all these things, if not quite beyond dispute, are yet so nearly certain, that no philosophy which rejects them can hope to stand. Only within the scaffolding of these truths, only on the firm foundation of unyielding despair, can the soul's habitation henceforth be safely built.[2]

In the end, the atheistic view reduces the botanist from studying daffodils to fertilizing them, the scientist from measuring the "big bang" to becoming a small fizzle, and the geologist from investigat-

> *In the end, the atheistic view reduces the botanist from studying daffodils to fertilizing them, the scientist from measuring the "big bang" to becoming a small fizzle, and the geologist from investigating the geological column to becoming embedded in one of its layers.*

ing the geological column to becoming embedded in one of its layers. Is it any wonder that when H. G. Wells, the ardent evolutionist and disciple of Huxley, saw at the very end of his life all his humanistic optimism crash in disaster, he wrote his last book, which is nothing less than a scream of despair. Malcolm Muggeridge poignantly described Wells's heart-rending gasp:

> Wells turned his face to the wall, letting off in *Mind at the End of Its Tether*, one last, despairing, whimpering cry which unsaid everything he had ever thought or hoped. Belatedly, he understood that what he had followed as a life-force was, in point of fact, a death wish, into which he was glad to sink the little that remained of his own life in the confident expectation of total and final obliteration.[3]

But human beings are too thoughtful to succumb to such a disastrous and know-nothing view of life. Every fiber within us cries out that there must be more than this.

Relationships Ruptured

At different junctures in life we feel the dark shadow of death, and our hearts cry out to know what it all means. There are several reasons for this. First, death is the severance of all relationships, with a sense of finality. Life may have its dreams, hopes, aspirations, and accomplishments, but in the long run, our lives are really built on some strong bond of relationship with significant others. To have this relationship threatened by sickness or temporary partings is endurable. But to face a separation that is final, and often sudden, seems to put life in the hands of some sharp, implacable hostility controlling our destinies.

Simone de Beauvoir described her mother's death "as violent and unforeseen as an engine stopping in the middle of the sky." All the glory of an individual is suddenly reduced to a cold piece of clay, and the mind that once brought to birth ideas and machines is now extinct.

Alfred Lord Tennyson wrote his poem "In Memoriam A.H.H." after the sudden death of his friend Arthur Hallam. In that protracted masterpiece written over several years, Tennyson, through the process of grieving, struggled to know what ultimate power manages the fate of humanity.

I have quoted several stanzas here to reveal the depth of his struggle and his realization of the philosophical implications from the choice between atheism and God. In the early part of the poem, with bitter submission, he voiced a veiled hostility toward God.

> Thine are these orbs of light and shade;
>   Thou madest Life in man and brute;
>   Thou madest Death; and lo, thy foot
> Is on the skull which thou hast made.

Several stanzas later his great struggle emerges as he alternates between God and nature, deeming first the one and then the other in control.

> Are God and Nature then at strife,
>   That Nature lends such evil dreams?
>   So careful of the type she seems,
> So careless of the single life, . . .
>
> "So careful of the type?" but no.
>   From scarpéd cliff and quarried stone
>   She cries, "A thousand types are gone;
> I care for nothing, all shall go.
>
> "Thou makest thine appeal to me:
>   I bring to life, I bring to death;
>   The spirit does but mean the breath:
> I know no more." And he, shall he,
>
> Man, her last work, who seemed so fair,
>   Such splendid purpose in his eyes,
>   Who rolled the psalm to wintry skies,
> Who built him fanes of fruitless prayer,
>
> Who trusted God was love indeed
>   And love Creation's final law—
>   Though Nature, red in tooth and claw
> With ravine, shriek'd against his creed—
>
> Who loved, who suffered countless ills,
>   Who battled for the True, the Just,

Be blown about the desert dust,
Or sealed within the iron hills?

No more? A monster then, a dream,
    A discord. Dragons of the prime,
    That tare each other in their slime,
Were mellow music matched with him.

O life as futile, then, as frail!
    O for thy voice to soothe and bless!
    What hope of answer, or redress?
Behind the veil, behind the veil.[4]

Tennyson's struggle is an "evolutionary" battle that predates the Darwinian thesis. It painfully raises the question of whether mindless nature is indeed our primordial soup. Notice carefully the vivid expressions of emotional struggle in a theoretical philosophy where God does not exist. Of Nature he says, "So careful of the type she seems, So careless of the single life." How can there be a larger "purpose" with no individual "purpose"? That is really the question.

But also notice the counterpoint he makes to that idea. Has Nature truly been that careful of the "type," or did it really emasculate several others as humans emerged by imitating Nature, "red in tooth and claw"? These questions deliver a mortal wound to athe-

> *Hope cannot be smuggled in*
> *by the naturalist's word game.*

ism because men and women, in naturalism's view, have survived by "tearing each other in their slime."

As profoundly as Tennyson deals with these issues, he finds two deductions to be unshakable: our relationships severed by death produce a heart of agony, and our destiny is bound up with our origin. Hope cannot be smuggled in by the naturalist's word game.

In the children's film *Prancer* we witness a very tender scene. The little girl in the lead role, Jessie, has recently lost her mother and converses with her friend. The friend asserts that she cannot believe in anything she cannot see. "But what about God?" says Jessie. "You can't see him, either. Does that mean you don't believe in him?" Her friend confesses her doubts about God for the same reason, and a surprised and agitated Jessie replies, "But if there's no God, there's no heaven. And if there's no heaven, then what about my mother?"

The human heart yearns for a meeting again, someday. And death just cannot destroy that longing. The Romantic poet William Wordsworth (1770–1850), in his poem "We Are Seven" speaks of this expression of the human heart.

> . . . I met a little cottage Girl:
> She was eight years old, she said:
> Her hair was thick with many a curl
> That clustered round her head. . . .
>
> "Sisters and brothers, little Maid,
> How many may you be?"
> "How many? Seven in all," she said,
> And wondering looked at me.
>
> "And where are they? I pray you tell."
> She answered, "Seven are we,
> And two of us at Conway dwell
> And two are gone to sea.
>
> "Two of us in the churchyard lie,
> My sister and my brother;
> And in the churchyard cottage, I
> Dwell near them with my mother. . . ."
>
> "You run about, my little Maid,
> Your limbs they are alive;
> If two are in the churchyard laid,
> Then ye are only five. . . ."
>
> "How many are you then," said I,
> "If they two are in heaven?"
> Quick was the little Maid's reply,
> "O master! we are seven."
>
> "But they are dead; those two are dead!
> Their spirits are in heaven!"

'Twas throwing words away; for still
The little Maid would have her will,
And said, "Nay, we are seven!"[5]

The idea that a relationship can be severed with such finality finds
no friendly reception, even in the mind of a child. However, this is
not the only question death raises for which we crave an answer;
there are other questions invoked by the mind. What about final
justice, if death is the end of all things?

Justice Jeopardized

English poet and author William Shenstone (1714–1763), in
one of his essays, complained that laws are generally found to be
nets of such a texture that the *little* creep through, the *great* break
through, and the *middle-sized* are entangled in them. If one were
to add up the unsolved crimes over the centuries, the question of
justice only looms larger. In our present day, it has been said that
in some nations (where, for the sake of security, homes are turned
into fortresses) the guilty walk free, while the innocent live behind
bars.

Winston Churchill spoke for the whole tormented world when
he cried for justice in pursuing the tormentor.

> I have only one purpose, the destruction of Hitler, and my life is much
> simplified, thereby. If Hitler invaded Hell, I would make at least a
> favorable reference to the Devil in the House of Commons.[6]

Anyone who saw the courtroom scene during the trial of Adolf
Eichmann will never forget when a cry for justice resounded from
the ranks of the onlookers. Life nudges us in our consciences with
its still, small voice that justice must be done if not in this world,
then in the world to come. Hence, the question rages in our hearts
whether death ends that possibility for justice—or guarantees it.

So strong is this instinct in human beings to believe that death,
and that which follows after death, are indispensable to balance
out this world of wrong, that even atheistic religions, such as Bud-

dhism, and monistic ones, such as Hinduism, invoke the Karmic law to work out evil and prosper the good. They cannot keep silent on the evils so evident.

Probably no one felt this issue of justice more deeply than did Job, with his deep commitment to God. In the biblical narrative, he lost his family, his wealth, and his health. Finally, his three friends arrived to inundate him with words which, summarized in one sentence, meant, "You are getting your due reward, Job." But Job argued repeatedly for his innocence. While the book, purpose, and teaching of Job go far deeper than my present application, it is, nevertheless, significant to note that at one point Job cried out, "If a man die, will he live again?" Somehow Job felt that the introduction of the right answer here had everything to do with justice and could mitigate his suffering.

If it is not the specifics of a ruptured love, or the unsatisfied hunger for the balances to be set straight, there is that which Solomon so well described:

> He has made everything beautiful in its time. He has also set eternity in the hearts of men; yet, they cannot fathom what God has done from the beginning to the end (Eccl. 3:11–12).

Herein is the tension, says Solomon: God has put eternity in our hearts. Yet, we cannot fathom the beginning from the end. This is the classic heart-mind conflict. Human beings, in their hearts, yearn for eternity, or at least sense the need for an eternal knowledge not bound by death. But our minds cannot deliver it. So ingrained is this yearning within us that to children death is an intrusion that has to be explained. They cannot conceive of a life relegated to a memory. Somehow, the eternity within the heart militates against the finality within their experience.

At least one other reason why death casts its long shadow over every human being is the deeply felt anxiety that death *may not* be the end, and that judgment will become a reality. For some this turns into an obsessive fear; for others it remains a sporadic concern. Every religion in the world staves off the possibility of judgment with carefully planned ceremonies and duties performed at the burial of the dead, and certain rites of passage that must not be violated.

The questions about death demand answers, but atheism has none because there is no heaven to be gained and no hell to be shunned. Life finishes with the last heartbeat: all relationships are severed, all endeavors are ended, the arm of justice is cut short, eternity in the heart has been swallowed up by the finality of experience. There is nothing to fear or to hope for, no God to meet, and no hope to anticipate—all is truly and ultimately ended.

Hope Abandoned

Having killed God, the atheist is left with no reason for being, no morality to espouse, no meaning to life, and no hope beyond the grave. Significantly, the absence of future hope has an amazing capacity to reach into the present and eat away at the structure of life, as termites would a giant wooden foundation. Hope is that indispensable element that makes the present so important. The ath-

> *Having killed God, the atheist is left with no reason for being, no morality to espouse, no meaning to life, and no hope beyond the grave.*

lete labors with the hope of victory. The researcher works diligently in the hope of a breakthrough. Every human endeavor has a hope, and if life itself has none, the application is foreshortened and the now is squandered away in the absence of any future gains.

There is a complete sense of alienation in the world one hundred years after Nietzsche. It is this utterly morbid and hopeless philosophy that has sent many of our youth into a search for other realities. Those who do not have hope, in an effort to drown their despair, turn to drugs or alcohol or other experiments that they think will break this stranglehold of futility. The farcical and the absurd are hallmarks of a trapped society, devoid of all hope. Why have our young people turned to drugs in such large numbers, and why are they opting for other states of consciousness? It is because of the unbearable emptiness they face with a philosophy of life that offers no hope and no answers.

After writing *Brave New World*, Aldous Huxley spent the latter years of his life seeking other realities in drugs. Huxley is the one who, in his book *Island*, had his hero say, "What a comfort to be in a place where the Fall [of man] is an exploded doctrine." After wrenching the past from the hands of a divine Creator, we barter away the present, convinced that there is nothing to hope for in the future. The eclectic composer John Cage recalled a lecture in which the New York painter, Willem de Kooning, responded to a questioner by saying, "The past does not influence me. I influence it." By rewriting the past, we have changed its influence on us. Our generation has nothing to look forward to but oblivion. The entailments of this are terrifying: cloning, drugs, AIDS, suicide and euthanasia, alcoholism, broken homes, crime, child pornography, terrorism, and a host of other problems that are heartbreaking. It is a short step from the "exploded" doctrines of the past to the disintegration of hope for the future.

Indeed, one author has observed:

In the 1950s, kids lost their innocence. They were liberated from their parents by well-paying jobs, cars, and lyrics in music that gave rise to a new term—the generation gap.

In the 1960s, kids lost their authority. It was the decade of protest—church, state, and parents were all called into question and found wanting. Their authority was rejected, yet nothing ever replaced it.

In the 1970s, kids lost their love. It was the decade of me-ism, dominated by hyphenated words beginning with self: self-image, self-esteem, self-assertion. It made for a lonely world. Kids learned everything there was to know about sex but forgot everything there was to know about love, and no one had the nerve to tell them there was a difference.

In the 1980s, kids lost their hope. Stripped of innocence, authority, and love, and plagued by the horror of a nuclear nightmare, large and growing numbers of this generation stopped believing in the future.[7]

I would add that in the 1990s, we lost our ability to reason. The power of critical thinking has gone from induction to deduction and very few are able to think clearly anymore. I have often said the challenge of the truth speaker today is this: How do you reach a generation that listens with its eyes and thinks with its feelings?

Our young people today are living with deep-seated fears because of all they see around them and feel within them. One young man, a friend of an acquaintance of mine, longing for some hope, some dream to cling to that would transcend the fetters of this world, found no answer from the world that had killed God. He chased other realities that only enmeshed him in deeper enslavements. His hopelessness represents a malady of all our youth who cry out for hope but find none in this Nietzschean world. This young man finally ended it all, but not before baring his heart in pathetic sentiments:

> Lost in the world of darkness
>   without a guiding light,
> Seeking a friend to help
>   my struggling, failing plight.
> Now all of you good people
>   just go on passing by,
> Leaving me with nothing
>   but this lonely will to die.
>
> Somewhere in this lonely world of sorrow and of woe
> There's a place for me to hide,
>   but where I do not know;
> For no matter where I go I never will escape
> The devil's reaching, clutching hands,
>   or the drink of fermented grape.
>
> So out of my grief and anguish
> Perhaps some wandering boy will see,
>   long after I have left this world,
> And build his own life, strong and good and free.

Nietzsche's character, "the madman" (in his parable by the same title) said that maybe his time had not yet come. Judging by the anguish of our youth, his time has come, and he has arrived. Atheism has borne this offspring, and it is her legitimate child—with no mind to look back to for his origin, no law to turn to for guidance, no meaning to cling to for life, and no hope for the future.

This is the shattered visage of atheism. It has the stare of death, looking into the barren desert of emptiness and hopelessness. Thus, the Nietzschean dogma, which dawned with the lantern being smashed to the ground, now ends in the darkness of the grave.

Questions for Study and Discussion

1. Explain what Albert Camus meant when he remarked that death is philosophy's only problem. Is this an understatement?
2. Read the excerpt from Alfred Lord Tennyson's "In Memoriam A.H.H." again. (You might even want to read the entire poem since Tennyson, who was a Christian, wrestles here with many of the ideas in this book. You can find it in several anthologies or online at http://tennysonpoetry.home.att.net/index.htm, where many of his other works are also available.) Describe your response to this poem. Do you think an atheist and a theist would respond differently or perhaps the same to this poem?
3. The author summarizes his four main points about atheism—in relation to origin, morality, meaning, and destiny—when he writes, "Having killed God, the atheist is left with no reason for being, no morality to espouse, no meaning to life, and no hope beyond the grave." Comment further on these four critical points and atheism's attempt to address them.

PART 2
GOD

The Treasure of Life's Pursuits

The pursuit of the perfect, then, is the pursuit of sweet-ness and light.

—Matthew Arnold

6

CLIMBING IN THE MIST

Truth, of course, must be stranger than fiction, for we have made fiction to suit ourselves.

—G. K. Chesterton

It is far better to debate a question before settling it than to settle a question before debating it. While the process does not always guarantee an inerrant conclusion, it often protects against vacuous leaps from ignorance to ignorance. Surely the high stakes involved in matters of life and destiny demand a response that is cohesive systematically and meaningful existentially. Nothing is as important as the truth, and no knowledge so dangerous as a lie, in an issue of such high import.

For this very reason, many thinking individuals go through a great personal struggle. They know that they must choose amid the cacophony of voices that lure from without and the divergent drives that impel from within. And often, those voices transpose harmonious sounds into discordant ones because of their prejudices and misconceptions.

Christianity, for example, has suffered much at the hands of its detractors, who have framed it as a mindless mass of material that strains credulity. Distortions and contrivances abound as some scholars have manipulated the Bible into pronouncements as far-fetched as specifying the age of the earth. Having erected a straw man, they demolish it with ease. Scholars once said that their task was one of "demythologizing," that is, removing so-called myths from the biblical text. But so bent upon the destruction of the Bible were some that when the "myths" were not to be found, they superimposed some of their own upon the text and drew inferences from them that were never intended. They constrained the text into their predisposed conclusions.

Yet rather than lay all the blame on its critics, a greater tragedy is the way the Christian faith has suffered at the hands of its supposed defenders. From bishops attired in ecclesiastical regalia disavowing the virgin birth, to the commercialized version of Christianity offering dolls for donations, the honest seeker does not know whether to laugh or cry. The marketplace of ideas is no longer analogous to a bazaar where one barters for one's soul, but is more akin to an auction where one is bidding for the least bizarre, so that he or she may return home without the feeling of being duped. Amid the confusion of so many beliefs, and the almost circus-like atmosphere of some so-called religious offerings, a person is not only overwhelmed but apprehensive. He thinks he can at best select that which is the least ridiculous. The great danger of such cynicism is the false conclusion that the truth about God can never be known.

Finding ourselves in this swirling cosmos, this matter of God's existence and life's proportionate meaning must be settled by each of us. Thankfully, as we climb in the mist, we are not without road signs. The nineteenth-century poet Robert Browning has said:

> This world's no blot for us,
> Nor blank; it means intensely, and means good:
> To find its meaning is my meat and drink.

I have attempted to argue, as C. S. Lewis did, that to find their way, atheists must make sense out of a random first cause, denounce as immoral all moral denunciation, express meaningfully all meaning-lessness, and find security in hopelessness. This is a tall order, even for a wizard with words. Once involved in this battle for meaning, Lewis decided that he would surrender and let God be God. Engaged in a philosophical struggle, he could no longer make sense of life while attempting to sever Christianity from its claim to truth. Lewis was caught in a maze of different options, and though having become a convinced atheist, the persuasiveness of Christ and his message finally conquered the mind of this brilliant thinker. He, in turn, through his writings, went on to influence both child and scholar in large numbers. The person of C. S. Lewis himself is incidental to my argument, but what he said is germane. He typifies the struggle of many as they journey from atheism to Christianity. The mood and the moment of his Christian commitment is well captured in his autobiography *Surprised by Joy*. In one memorable description he wrote:

> To find their way, atheists must make sense out of a random first cause, denounce as immoral all moral denunciation, express meaningfully all meaninglessness, and find security in hopelessness. I had always wanted above all things, not to be "interfered with." I had wanted "to call my soul my own." I had been far more anxious to avoid suffering than to achieve delight. I had always aimed at limited liabilities. . . . You must picture me alone in that room in Magdalen, night after night, feeling, when ever my mind lifted even for a second from my work, the steady, unrelenting approach of him whom I so earnestly desired not to meet. That which I greatly feared had at last come upon me. In the Trinity Term of 1929 I gave in, and admitted that God was God, and knelt and prayed: perhaps, that night, the most dejected and reluctant convert in all England. I did not then see what is now the most shining and obvious thing; the Divine humility which will accept a convert even on such terms. The prodigal son at least walked home on his own feet. But who can duly adore that Love which will open the high gates to a prodigal who is brought in kicking, struggling, resentful, and darting his eyes in every direction for a chance to escape? The words "compelle intrare," compel them to come in, have been so abused by wicked men that we shudder at them; but properly understood, they plumb the depth of the Divine mercy. The hardness of God is kinder than the softness of men, and his compulsion is our liberation.[1]

"Kicking and struggling" is indicative of the resistance Lewis put up because of his perception that Christianity was a thing to be shunned. "Resentful," he said, because he had fought it with great philosophical might, and the defeat of his arguments was not an easy admission. Yet, "surprised by joy," because, for the first time, as he breathed the mountain air of spiritual reality, life was brought into focus.

How does one move from atheism to Christ? It is a steep climb. Every step matters, for the slide downward becomes unstoppable. Contrast, for example, the sentiments of C. S. Lewis with those of Eugene O'Neill, the famed American dramatist. His plays are unquestionably some of the finest of our time. One of his friends, noticing a preoccupation in the themes O'Neill addressed, said, "For O'Neill, the quest has always been for God." Yet, if his play *Long Day's Journey into Night* is truly autobiographical, he did not find God. His remorse is evidenced in the sad conclusion of the play, in the words of the mother facing the events driving her and others toward disaster.

> None of us can help the things life has done to us. They are done before you realize it, and once they are done, they make you do other things until, at last, everything comes between you and what you'd like to be, and you've lost your true self forever.

O'Neill, perhaps speaking of himself through the character of the son, said that only on certain occasions at sea did he ever feel "the joy of belonging to a fulfillment beyond men's lousy, pitiful, greedy fears, and hopes, and dreams."

Whatever promptings in our minds O'Neill's words might make, there is no mistaking the manifest difference in the two autobiographical titles, *Surprised by Joy* and *Long Day's Journey into Night*. It is the difference God makes.

How, then, does one rise to the perspective that sustains this point? In the words of Mao Tse Tung, no friend of theism, "Even the Great March had to begin with a first step."

The Possible Roads

The starting point has to be an understanding of the process by which we come to affirm beliefs as true or false. How does any individual human being, as a subject in this world of conflicting claims, relate to objects around him and arrive at a correct understanding of reality? This issue has occupied philosophy from the beginning of time and is the decisive first step to knowledge. An error here will only be multiplied in the distant pursuits of every branch of learning, just as a slight error in a computer's database can be compounded. An erroneous starting point snarls the journey into truth.

Professor Colin Gunton began his excellent book *Enlightenment and Alienation* with the question, "What happens when we perceive, or think that we perceive, the sights and sounds, textures, tastes and smells of the world in which we live? On the answer to that question depend the answers to all kinds of questions."[2]

This pursuit of truth is nowhere near as simple as it may at first appear, for it brings into the context of decision-making the nature of reality (which outwardly changes), the kinds of reality (material world, realm of thought, etc.), and the ways of knowing (the senses or the mind). In short, the mist can get quite thick. It would be very easy, here, to digress into distant terrain and begin an intense philosophical battle with representatives of the different schools of thought. Between the two extremes of Rationalism (the quest for indubitable rational certainty) and Fideism (which roots all knowledge in faith) there comes an avalanche of other methods, each in its own way claiming to have reached the truth. These include Agnosticism, Experientialism, Evidentialism, Pragmatism, and Combinationalism. The last of these categories I will be discussing later.[3]

Rational certainty has always been that glittering dome, imagined or otherwise, on the huge edifice of philosophy. The modern father of the quest for rational certainty is René Descartes. He found his starting point in *cogito ergo sum*—"I think, therefore, I am." David Hume chiseled the statement down further and said we must eliminate the "I" and reach an even more fundamental assertion: "I think, therefore thinking exists." Hans Driesch, Danish biologist, went one better and said, "I am something (I can't be sure of what) at this very moment when I raise this question."[4] All this is reminiscent of the student at New York University who intimidatingly asked the question of his professor, "Sir, how do

I know that I exist?" A lingering pause preceded the professor's answer. He lowered his glasses, peered over the rim, and riveted his eyes on the student. His simple response finally came, "And whom shall I say is asking?" Fortunately or otherwise, some things in life are just undeniable.

Descartes placed supreme confidence in the power of unaided human reason. Employing the method of doubt and applied mathematics, he envisioned a complete fundamental science of nature, demonstrable with mathematical certainty. The mind to him was like a box into which, and by the limitations of which, reality would be encompassed. Descartes sought a firm foundation of knowledge built on the doubting capacity of the mind. From that he would build with the blocks of clear words, distinct ideas, and concepts whose meaning was determinate. But this Cartesian position, pushed to an extreme, paid a dear price in its attempt to pass from the mist-filled valley of doubt to the mountain of clear knowledge.[5] That price was a diminished or destroyed confidence in the senses. In a reaction to this the British empiricists came on the scene and gave priority to sense experience.

The quest for rational certainty is admirable, and it is imperative that the shortcomings of this ideal not diminish some of its strength. The role of reason is pivotal and cannot be lost in the final checklist of a worldview. For now, however, I just want to point out the counter side of this approach and bring a necessary caution. It is impossible, when dealing with all of reality, to force mathematical certainty into every test for truthfulness. Life is just not livable that way, and in fact, science would collapse if it consistently believed that at every step. Einstein himself challenged this illusory certainty in mathematics, saying, "As far as the propositions of mathematics refer to reality, they are not certain; and as far as they are certain, they do not refer to reality."[6] It would be better to describe our pursuit as that which seeks a high degree of certainty, or meaningful certainty. A meaningful and high degree of certainty, rather than mathematical certainty, is more attainable.

We must recognize that a person comes to reality not from a single strand of truth testing, but from a convergence of one's own multifaceted framework. Every life is an admixture of the rationality of the mind, the intimations from the senses, the influences of the imagination, and the commitments of the will. The struggle comes in knowing where and when each must operate. To mutilate man's process of knowing into these constituent parts, as if they operated independently of each other, is to disfigure him as a person and to destroy the nature of reality. If rational certainty were the only way, and all knowledge of reality could be affirmed only on the basis of critical analysis by the mind, then a child could never know and experience God. Is this not one of the suicidal leaps of pantheism, where religion has become so sophisticated and obscure that it is

> *It is impossible, when dealing with all of reality, to force mathematical certainty into every test for truthfulness.*

only within the exclusive domain of the scholar to understand who we are? Hence, the debates of many Eastern philosophies often confuse terms and incomprehensible concepts in attempting to understand what we mean when we talk about "self."

Once again I state that the role of reason is foundational and how it functions is indispensable to a tenable worldview. Reason tells us that human beings are composites. Any attempt to dislocate or reduce us prejudices the conclusion. The detached rationalist, however, could end up falling in love with one lonely, little truth. The exaltation of relational certainty to dizzying heights as the sole arbiter of reality overshadows the individual. It is not at all surprising that alienation followed on the heels of the Enlightenment. Where rational certainty had become the master, and the power of unaided reason held exclusive sway on truth, the masses felt alienated from the real world. The average human being does not discuss Kant and Descartes over dinner. The rigorous and contributive nature of their systems notwithstanding, a high and wide wall has been erected that the masses will never be able to climb. In the face of such estrangement, and the sense of being shut out, existentialism (the power of the will to conquer despair) was waiting to be born. Can we forget the 1960s when university students, in many instances joined by the most well-known professors of the day, sat on the lawns of campuses, smoking pot and denouncing all authority? Sheer intellectual pursuit had failed.

Having said that, it is equally important for the pursuer of truth who approaches life purely from one's sense perception to observe the same caution. If the telescope proved anything, it warned us of the erroneous perceptual assumptions that we can make if perception reigns supreme, for it does not always reveal things as they are.

Maintaining Our Balance

If reality, then, impinges upon us in a multiplicity of ways, we need a paradigm or worldview that reasonably explains the truth-tested realities of this world, which can then be blended together to give life a composite unity.

Let me borrow an illustration from Francis Schaeffer to demonstrate the need for this approach. Suppose you were to leave a room with two glasses on the table, Glass A and Glass B. Glass A has two ounces of water in it, and Glass B is empty. When you return at the end of the day, Glass B now has water in it and Glass A is empty. You could assume that someone took the water from Glass A and put it into Glass B. That, however, does not fully explain the situation, because you notice that Glass B has four ounces of water in it, whereas Glass A had only two ounces in it when you left in the morning.

You are confronted with a problem that at best has only a partial explanation. Whether the water from Glass A was poured into Glass B is debatable. But what is beyond debate is that all of the water in Glass B could not have come from Glass A. The additional two ounces had to have come from elsewhere.

God has put enough into the world to make faith in him a most reasonable thing, and he has left enough out to make it impossible to live by sheer reason or observation alone. Science may be able to explain the two ounces in Glass B. It cannot explain the four ounces in it.

The Christian worldview, biblically based, presents a powerful and unique explanation of these other "two ounces." With remarkable persuasion, contemporary apologists have shown the theistic framework to be not only credible, but also far more adept than atheism in dealing with the real questions of philosophy.[7] With this as a foundation, the Christian worldview erects an equally persua-

> *God has put enough into the world to make faith in him a most reasonable thing, and he has left enough out to make it impossible to live by sheer reason or observation alone.*

sive superstructure. Whichever starting point we take—either the philosophical followed by the biblical or the biblical by itself, which for many is sufficient—the cogency and convincing power of the answers emerge very persuasively. The original "two ounces," as well as the additional "two ounces," are best explained in a theistic framework. The arguments range from the simple to the intricate, depending on the question and its context.

Jesus splendidly coalesced extremes in his earthly ministry by bringing balance and detail to truth. He mesmerized the lawyers, doctors, and religious teachers of the day with his authority and unassailable arguments. It was said of him that he left the scholar of the day amazed, but what was more, "the common people heard him gladly." Paul the rabbi, Luke the doctor, and Peter the fisherman, all grasped reality as they had never grasped it before when he opened the doors of their minds and hearts to the truth.

But herein lies the challenge. The one responding to the question is always torn between the need to satisfy the demands of the subject being dealt with and the capacity of the questioner to understand the concepts. Renowned Cambridge professor Stephen Hawking, for example, is commended for his gift in using the technical data of his expertise to explain the nature of the universe in a popular treatment. However, it does not take long for the reader to realize that the more penetrating the question, the more Hawking's answers elude even the highly trained.

Remembering the Goal

One needs to climb high enough to recognize that the mist has been dissolved, and yet not so high that one enters air too rarified to breathe. How may we know that we have reached such a vantage point? If we can clearly define our goal, then we will possess a way of ascertaining our position. And the goal may be best described as subjecting the intimations of reality to adequate truth tests so that one may arrive at a worldview that answers the questions of our origin, condition, salvation, and destiny. A worldview may be defined as the philosophical glasses that a person wears to look at this world of ideas, experiences, and purposes. The worldview functions as an interpretive conceptual scheme to explain why we "see" the world as we do and act as we do.[8]

Every individual has a worldview, either by design or default. Neutrality is an illusion. Implicit in what I am saying are two inescapable factors. First, that in order to withstand the scrutiny of truth, a worldview must have a mix of certain components. Second, a failure here leads to a faulty worldview with proportionate consequences. (The process involved in the defense and establishment of a credible worldview has been carefully explained in appendix 2.)

While we climb through the mist with our finite limitations and proneness to error, and attempt to reach this mountaintop of clear knowledge, the Bible categorically asserts the possibility of knowing the truth. God has spoken to us in many ways. He has not left himself without a witness. In fact, the Bible states that the evidence and manner of God's communication leaves us without excuse. However, one indispensable prerequisite to a pursuit of truth is the honesty of intent. A mind that is bent on suppressing or hindering the truth will ultimately find the lie it is chasing. Scottish author George MacDonald stated it succinctly, "To try to explain truth to him who loves it not is but to give him more plentiful material for misinterpretation."[9] Richard Weaver, former professor of English at the University of Chicago, reinforced the idea:

> How frequently it is brought to our attention that nothing good can be done if the will is wrong. Reason alone fails to justify itself.

... If the disposition is wrong, reason increases maleficence: if it is right, reason orders and furthers the good.[10]

Sustaining this idea of the proper attitude toward truth, Jesus pointed to a child as the illustration of the kingdom of heaven, not to the qualities of being childish and error prone, but to the sincerity and teachability of one with childlike innocence.

Scientific or philosophical pursuits, and a belief in God, ought not to be seen as contradictory approaches to reality. That assumption misunderstands their nature. It is not accidental that it has generally been in the milieu of Christian belief that investigation in science and thought have flourished. A love for God prompts a love for knowing the world that he has created. The quest for knowledge and truth, therefore, is not hindered, but guided by the very purposes of God. G. K. Chesterton said, "God is like the sun; you cannot look at it, but without it you cannot look at anything else."

How does God persuade multisensory human beings to come to the truth? Let us climb to see the view from above the mist, and penetrate its density through the eyes of God.

Questions for Study and Discussion

1. When moving from atheism to theism, the author argues, "The starting point has to be an understanding of the process by which we come to affirm beliefs as true or false." (For an extensive discussion on this process, see appendix 1.) How might you begin to think about this pursuit of truth in relation to faith? Is rational certainty an attainable or desirable goal?

2. Discuss the statement, "God has put enough into the world to make faith in him a most reasonable thing, and he has left enough out to make it impossible to live by sheer reason or observation alone." What does this tell us about who we are as multisensory human beings (i.e., cognitive, relational, etc.) and how we arrive at knowing God?

3. Explain what G. K. Chesterton meant when he wrote, "God is like the sun; you cannot look at it, but without it you cannot look at anything else." In light of Chesterton's conclusion, what are the implications for an atheistic worldview?

7

WITH LARGER EYES
THAN OURS

*The problem with Christianity is not that it has been
tried and found wanting, but that it has been found
difficult, and left untried.*

—G. K. Chesterton

A lecture I attended by Dr. Stephen Hawking was entitled
"Determinism: Is Man a Slave or the Master of His
Fate?" Anyone who has read Dr. Hawking's book *A
Brief History of Time* has seen him pictured on the back cover
in a wheelchair. Unfortunately, Dr. Hawking is a victim of Lou
Gehrig's disease. In his dreadful confinement, virtually all of his
capable activity is now in his mind. All physical capacities have
been eroded. I mention this only to raise the question: How does
one with no voice deliver a lecture?

The process itself is fascinating. Placed before him in his wheelchair that day was an apparatus that represents the genius of
modern-day technology. The hardware and software facilitate his
word selection and sentence formations, which are then rendered

audible through a speech synthesizer. The speech synthesizer was developed by one of California's prestigious schools, prompting a humorous introduction by Dr. Hawking, as he apologized to his English audience for his American accent.

Even more amazing is that Dr. Hawking is able to manage this entire process by the motion of one finger, which is restricted to a minuscule movement of one millimeter. Should this finger ultimately be immobile to even that extent, there is a secondary capacity, through the sending of an infrared beam into the eye. Blinking the eye would interrupt the beam, and signal the selection process. Aided by this equipment, either with the blink of an eye or the movement of a finger, one of the world's most noted scientists could transfer thought into audible speech. All of his content would be of no use without this masterpiece of a machine to give him vocal capacities, while his body and muscle functions are inoperative.

One of the most intriguing aspects of the afternoon was to watch this process and listen to this phenomenal thinker discussing whether we are the random products of chance, and hence, not free, or whether God had designed these laws within which we are free. I had to wonder if any person could have left that crowded lecture hall wondering whether this incredible piece of equipment used by Dr. Hawking was designed or had randomly come about! It had taken humanity at its finest to design something with such capability.

1. In the Beginning—GOD

Nobody in his right mind would ever believe that a dictionary developed because of an explosion in a printing press. Every designed product in the human experience points to a designer. The argument is literally and figuratively as old as the hills. That is why it does not matter how loudly the intellectual community shouts "Chance!" They have not been able to conquer the dreadful void of determinism and end up giving designed arguments to argue against design. Science is unconvincing when trying to establish how personality can come from non-personality. It does not know how to cope with the diversity of effect if there is a unity of the first cause. Human sexuality is not satisfactorily or sensibly explained by mindless evolution. The intricacies and fulfillment of human affections make randomness a senseless argument.

Man on the Witness Stand

The argument from design is the very approach God used with Job. Job had become weary of his pain and sought a just answer for it. The constant implication of Job's questioning was that he already "knew" so much and needed to "know" why he, an innocent man, was suffering. As the story unfolded, Job threw a flurry of questions at his philosopher friends, who valiantly tried to answer him. But they could not have been more off the mark. God then broke his silence, challenging Job's very assumptions and reminding him that there was an awful lot Job did not know but had just accepted and believed by inference. Notice the beauty and detail with which God appeals to Job on the intricacies of this universe. God, in effect, said, "All right, Job. Since you only accept that which you comprehensively understand, let me toss a few questions your way."

> Then the LORD answered Job out of the storm.
> He said:
>
> Who is it that darkens my counsel
>   with words without knowledge?
> Brace yourself like a man;
> I will question you,
>   and you will answer me.
>
> Where were you when I laid the earth's foundation?
>   Tell me, if you understand.
> Who marked off its dimensions? Surely you know!
>   Who stretched a measuring line across it?
> On what were its footings set,
>   or who laid its cornerstone . . .
>
> Who shut up the sea behind doors
>   when it burst forth from the womb,
> when I made the clouds its garment
>   and wrapped it in thick darkness,

when I fixed limits for it
    and set its doors and bars in place,
when I said, "This far you may come and no farther;
    here is where your proud waves halt"? . . .

Have you journeyed to the springs of the sea
    or walked in the recesses of the deep?
Have the gates of death been shown to you? . . .

What is the way to the abode of light?
    And where does darkness reside?
Can you take them to their places? . . .

Have you entered the storehouses of the snow
    or seen the storehouses of the hail,
which I reserve for times of trouble,
    for days of war and battle?
What is the way to the place where the lightning is dispersed,
    or the place where the east winds are scattered over the earth?
Who cuts a channel for the torrents of rain,
    and a path for the thunderstorm,
to water a land where no man lives,
    a desert with no one in it,
to satisfy a desolate wasteland
    and make it sprout with grass?
Does the rain have a father?
    Who fathers the drops of dew?
From whose womb comes the ice?
    Who gives birth to the frost from the heavens
when the waters become hard as stone,
    when the surface of the deep is frozen?

Can you bind the beautiful Pleiades?
    Can you loose the cords of Orion?
Can you bring forth the constellations in their seasons
    or lead out the Bear with its cubs?
Do you know the laws of the heavens?
    Can you set up God's dominion over the earth? . . .

Who endowed the heart with wisdom
    or gave understanding to the mind?

Do you hunt the prey for the lioness
    and satisfy the hunger of the lions

when they crouch in their dens
    or lie in wait in a thicket?
Who provides food for the raven
    when its young cry out to God
and wander about for lack of food? . . .

The LORD said to Job:
Will the one who contends with the Almighty correct him?
    Let him who accuses God answer him!

Job 38:1–40:2

In sixty-four questions God presented Job with the great mysteries of this tightly-knit universe, at once intelligible and mysterious. For Job, the splendor was now too great to miss. The designer who had designed this world could also bring design out of Job's suffering. He was now willing to see the purpose for all of life through the eyes of God.

When we of lesser sight see with 20/20 vision, our understanding is completely changed, as the following story shows.

> While traveling to Chicago by train, I sat behind a man and his young son. The boy seemed intrigued by the passing scenery and described to his father everything that he saw. He talked about some children at play in a school yard.
>
> He mentioned the rocks in a small stream and described the sunlight's reflection on the water. When we stopped for a freight train to cross our track, the boy tried to guess what each car might be hauling. As we neared the city he expressed excitement over the waves of Lake Michigan and told about the many boats in dry dock. At the end of the trip I leaned forward and said to the father, "How refreshing to enjoy the world through the eyes of a child!" He smiled and replied, "Yes, it is. Especially if it's the only way you can see it." He was blind.

The atheist misses this glimpse through larger eyes than his own. Such a person is confronted in life with a universe that is intelligible and mysterious. But, in the despotism of his naturalistic worldview, such a person attempts to remove the mystery and only succeeds in decimating the intelligence. The atheist's prejudice against miracles robs him of the miraculous nature of the world itself. By denying the possibility of a miracle, he does not really solve the dilemma of origins, for a slow miracle ought to be just as incredible as a swift one.[1]

The story is told of a man who was fishing. Every time he caught a large fish he threw it away, and each time he caught a small one he kept it. An exasperated onlooker, watching this strange process of selection, asked him what, in reason's name, he was doing. The

> *By denying the possibility of a miracle, he does not really solve the dilemma of origins, for a slow miracle ought to be just as incredible as a swift one.*

man just blinked and said, "I only have an eight-inch frying pan, and so the larger ones won't fit!"

This story is only a humorous version of the old Greek legend of the innkeeper who had a bed of very restrictive size. Whenever he had a guest who was too tall, he just sawed off the extending limbs.

Any event that strains the naturalist's ability to explain is re-sized to fit one's own prejudice. Hence, the naturalist prefers to conclude that bacteria, shuttled in by a guided missile, began life in this world.

In Psalm 19, David reminds us that the splendor of the universe is the handiwork and expression of God:

> The heavens declare the glory of God;
>   the skies proclaim the work of his hands.
> Day after day they pour forth speech;
>   night after night they display knowledge.
> There is no speech or language
>   where their voice is not heard.
> Their voice
>   goes out into all the earth,
>   their words to the ends of the world.

The apostle Paul expressed this same theme to confirm that in creation, as well as within the human mind, God's eternal power is manifested (Rom. 1:20). God has spoken from without and from within, but human beings, determined on their self-indulgent paths, repress the truth and miss the imprint of God.

The tragedy of the atheist is really twofold. Not only do his efforts fail to yield the consummate knowledge that he chases, but also, in his insatiable appetite to know, he intrudes into areas that ultimately deny him a sense of awe and the thrill of contentment.

Breaking the Hold of Determinism

The Christian approaches knowledge from a drastically different point of view. The Christian sees human beings as created by God in a very unique situation from which to relate to the world. The best description of this is "semitranscendence." One retains this both in relation to oneself and to the world. Only a divine Creator could explain this capacity that is necessary, if one's postulations about oneself and one's world are to be trusted. The late Colin Gunton, one of the most significant voices in British theology, explained this very important vantage point:

> We stand neither God-like over the material world, as the rationalism of the Enlightenment has encouraged us to think, nor at the mercy of something utterly different and incomprehensible, as some forms of existentialist reaction to rationalism may suggest. We can know the world, though not infallibly, nor with an aim at a kind of omniscience, because we are both part of it and able to transcend it through our personal powers of perception, imagination and reason. . . . Man is not God—not omnipotent or omniscient—but part of that which is created. On the other hand, there is a transcendence of the other creatures: made in the "image and likeness of God," to rule the earth not after the paradigm of modern technocracy, but as a gardener over his garden, and always under God.[2]

Michael Polanyi, philosopher of science, in his landmark work *Personal Knowledge*, sustained the same idea of semitranscendence. He pointed out how the openness of the world to our personal knowing points to the reality of God. The Christian is, therefore, free from determinism on the one hand and total transcendence on the other. The atheist is trapped by either one or the other.

Someone has said, "If you want to hear God laugh, tell him your plans." It might be added, "If you want to hear him laugh even louder, tell him what you know." In the light of that, Robert Jastrow's astute observation in his book *God and the Astronomers* may well have identified the last laugh. Dealing with the question of the book of Genesis and science, Jastrow, a scientist with extraordinary credentials and a one-time director of NASA's Goddard Institute for Space Studies, said:

> The details differ, but the essential elements in the astronomical and biblical accounts of Genesis are the same. . . .
> This is an exceedingly strange development, unexpected by all but the theologians. They have always believed the word of the Bible. But we scientists did not expect to find evidence for an abrupt beginning because we have had, until recently, such extraordinary success in tracing the chain of cause and effect backward in time. . . .
> At this moment it seems as though science will never be able to raise the curtain on the mystery of creation. For the scientist who has lived by his faith in the power of reason, the story ends like a bad dream. He has scaled the mountains of ignorance; he is about to conquer the highest peak; as he pulls himself over the final rock, he is greeted by a band of theologians who have been sitting there for centuries.[3]

For the Christian, the acknowledgment of God as the Creator of life brings to bear one very significant life-transforming truth. The Bible makes it specific that God, in his love, created us. Thus, it is not life that precedes love, but love that precedes life. It is the love of God that gave us life in creation, just as it is the love of a mother that enables a child to live in procreation. Any attempt to thwart the love of God thwarts his design and brings discord in life because it rejects the very motivation in the creation of life.

One can readily see how the failure to implement the role of love has resulted in modern society becoming the most abortive of life in all of history. The opposite of love is selfishness, and the rights of the one bearing the baby have now eradicated the love needed to give life. From "live and let live," we have moved to "live and let die." Love is creation's first law, and if love has preceded life, then for life to succeed, it must live within the boundaries of this love.

2. The Sovereignty of Good

The second major affirmation of theism, which is powerfully sustained in the human experience, is the intrinsically moral nature of the universe. If love is creation's first law, it is consistent within that framework to delineate love's boundaries—this is the moral law. A failure to understand the nature of love has resulted in our inability to appreciate a moral framework. We find ourselves bewildered by love's entailments and we wallow in the muddy waters of sensual indulgence. A foundational fallacy about love doubly jeopardizes one's experience, for in squandering the purity of love, one also forfeits true liberty. In its stead, one grasps at poor substi-

> *The second major affirmation of theism, which is powerfully sustained in the human experience, is the intrinsically moral nature of the universe.*

tutes that leave one enslaved by insatiable cravings. In resisting the legitimate terms of endearment, one is left encrusted by a hardening layer that morality cannot penetrate. He or she has spurned true love, and in doing so has banished from one's experience virtues indispensable to survival.

G. K. Chesterton vividly expressed this:

> They have invented a new phrase, a phrase that is a black and white contradiction in two words—"free love"—as if a lover ever had been, or ever could be, free. It is the nature of love to bind itself, and the institution of marriage merely paid the average man the compliment of taking him at his word.[4]

Chesterton identified well the necessary assumptions in any honorable relationship: virtue, trust, and commitment. Without these, no human intercourse of any value is possible. But somehow, in our day, we have come to the conclusion that unaided reason can fashion a moral law. This has clearly proven to be wrong, and we are the hapless inhabitants of cities that are self-destructing and homes that are breaking apart in epidemic proportions. In the name of freedom, we have been handcuffed by fear and immoral enslavements. We must deal with this or die.

So pivotal is the nature of morality to life itself that the Bible equates life with moral uprightness and death with the absence of moral sensitivity. It is for this reason that the first recorded communication between God and man following creation was on the nature of good and evil. How far we have strayed from God's original pattern is seen in our present-day delegitimatization of morality. Our educators have convinced themselves that the unexamined life can be virtuous, and our teachers are under strict injunctions to shun moral instruction.

The Painful Malady

Studying this moral confusion from any moment in history, particularly in societies where freedom is procured, it is not difficult to sense the points of tension. To understand where these tensions are felt most is essential because such knowledge will direct us toward an understanding of the problem. Once that is grasped, the clear perspective of the Christian faith can be seen.

The atheist feels the sharp edges of moral demands on at least three points. The first, and foremost, is the arena of law. Nobody senses the moral struggle we are facing more than the lawmakers of the land, whether they be atheists or theists. They find themselves unavoidably playing God in a society that wants everything, but with no moral obligation to anyone, except as one's own conscience dictates. The dilemma is not too difficult to enunciate; it is the solution that seems forever elusive. People find themselves in society as individuals having necessarily to live in harmony with other individuals. There rises inexorably the agonizing conflict between individual rights and societal responsibility. A person thus approaches the problem nervously, like the proverbial donkey between two stacks of hay. However, such a person is afraid to diminish either, as it would violate the rules. Thus, the individual arrives at a well-worded principle that is thought to dispel the problem:

> The love of liberty, liberty for all without distinction of class, creed, or country, and the resolute preference of the interests of the whole to any interest, be it what it may, of a narrower scope.[5]

These two principles—that is, of individual liberty and the good of the whole—undergird much of contemporary jurisprudence. But no sooner do we state the principles than the contradiction becomes evident. The absolute freedom of the individual cannot be guarded in the maze of society's collective interests. There is clearly liberty with distinction, and liberty ends up being redefined, depending upon the court in session.

Notice, moreover, that even before the problem of the contra-dictions is the moral assumption that freedom and fairness are *morally necessary*. Forgotten here is that natural selection must involve natural rejection—and who is going to be rejected. From whence have all these platitudes and truisms, that are so noble and tolerant, suddenly emerged? It is one thing to picture Lady Justice blindfolded with a balance in her hand; it is quite another to prove *why it is important* for the balance to be fair. The atheist has a gnawing feeling all along that the blindfold may protect the adjudicator from the tyranny of the eye, but he or she cannot escape the moral assumptions in the mind. The first point of tension, then, is the freedom of the individual versus society.

A second point of tension is over how the spheres of private life and public life overlap. The atheist believes that one's moral beliefs are a private matter and ought not to impinge upon one's public behavior or surface in one's public pronouncements. Morality is a dirty word in public, and immorality has no damning effect if it is kept private.

The atheist has convinced himself that private practices and public behavior are so morally unrelated that the individual can easily draw lines and cross borders without any dirt sticking to one's feet. Morality has become quarantined, and the watchdog of civil libertarianism has its security guards well-placed to make sure that you *do* leave home without it. While this position is fraught with insoluble problems, let me underscore just two.

Is not the very assumption that there can be a disjunction between my public and private life a moral presupposition? Further, this is the precise route of self-destruction that prompted Aristotle to raise the question, "Is democratic behavior behavior democracies like, or behavior that will preserve a democracy?"

Torn between the tension of individual freedom vis-à-vis societal responsibility and the tension of the private practice vis-à-vis public office, naturalism is dragged to the third dilemma. This is the unending pursuit of a unifying theory of ethics. E. L. Mascall, in his book *The Importance of Being Human*, worded the dilemma this way:

> Living like a gorilla is a very good thing to do if you are a gorilla, and living like an angel is a very good thing to do if you are an angel. And neither of these tasks is very difficult for the being in question. If, however, you are a human being you can achieve true happiness only by living as a human being, and that is a much more difficult task.

Ah! But there is the rub. "If, however, you are a human being you can achieve true happiness only living as a human being. . . ." But, with atheistic presuppositions we do not know what a human being is. How, then, may we know what is good for us? Thinking atoms discussing morality is absurd. Thus, all types of solutions ranging from Immanuel Kant's capacity of unaided reason to Joseph Fletcher's *Situation Ethics* collide in blatant contradictions. The extremes of position are well stated by Fletcher himself in a quote from Cicero in *de Legibus*:

> Only a madman could maintain that the distinction between the honorable and the dishonorable, between virtue and vice, is a matter of opinion, not of nature. [Fletcher commented], This is nevertheless, precisely and exactly what situation ethics maintains.[6]

What was lunacy to Cicero has become the sanest principle for Fletcher. Trying to balance virtue and vice has rocked our civilization so that we have become like a drunken man, reeling from one wall to the other, knocking himself senseless with every hit. The

> *Where the naturalistic worldview is assumed, it admits to an unknown starting point for life, and therefore, for morality as well.*

naturalist's ethic is not objective. Words such as *reality*, *human being*, *freedom*, and *justice* are not value-free. Ethics is reduced to sheer prescriptivism, or existential preference. Where the naturalistic worldview is assumed, it admits to an unknown starting point for life, and therefore, for morality as well.

A Definitive Diagnosis

The Christian answer is a strong counterperspective to naturalism—and rightly so, for it challenges human beings in their claim to absolute autonomy. As G. K. Chesterton observed, "We do not want a religion that is right where we are right. What we want is a religion that is right where we are wrong."

The atheist makes two very serious mistakes in his starting point for moral discussion: first, what morality is, and second, what purpose morality serves. He asserts that he can, by the power of unaided reason, arrive at the nature of morality and at a satisfactory moral law. So natural is the capacity of the mind, says Kant in his *Groundwork on Ethics*, that a person can turn away from a direct encounter with Christ, and, independent of Christ's influence, be able to reason through to the right conclusions. In *The Sovereignty of Good*, Iris Murdoch has a perfect response to this Kantian belief:

How recognizable, how familiar to us, is the man so beautifully portrayed in the *Groundwork*, who confronted even with Christ turns away to consider the judgment of his own conscience and to hear the voice of his own reason. . . . This man is with us still, free, independent, lovely, powerful, rational, responsible, brave, the hero of so many novels and books of moral philosophy. The "raison d'etre" of this attractive but misleading creature is not far to seek. He is the offspring of the age of science, confidently rational, and yet increasingly aware of his alienation from the material universe which his discoveries reveal . . . his alienation is without cure . . . It is not such a long step from Kant to Nietzsche to existentialism, and the Anglo-Saxon ethical doctrines which in some ways closely resemble it . . . In fact, Kant's man had already received a glorious incarnation nearly a century earlier in the work of Milton: his proper name is Lucifer.[7]

To be precise, this man is not post-scientific or incarnated for the first time in Milton's work. In fact, we meet him in the Garden of Eden, where he arrogated to himself the godlike characteristic of defining good and evil, and doing so apart from God. This reality is at the heart of the Christian argument for morality. It asserts not only the inevitable sense of alienation within any belief that places man as the measure of all things; it also defines what it means to be immoral. The word is "pride," "hubris"—an autonomy that wills its independence from God. Knowledge and education in the hands of one who claims no higher accountability or authority than one's own individuality is power in the hands of a fool. The English poet Alexander Pope said:

> Of all the causes which conspire to blind
> Man's erring judgment, and misguide the mind;
> What the weak head with strongest bias rules,—
> Is pride, the never-failing vice of fools.[8]

The French aristocrat Alexis de Tocqueville (1805–1859) was only half right when he said, during his voyage to England and Ireland:

> The French want no one to be their superior. The English want in-
> feriors. The French man constantly raises his eyes above him with

anxiety. The English man lowers his beneath him with satisfaction. On either side it is pride, but understood in a different way.[9]

The problem is not with the French or the English. It is with all mankind. None of us likes authority. It all began in the first days of creation, when the first man and woman refused to allow God to be God, and wanted to be as God themselves. Thus, sin entered the world through the rejection of God and the choice for autonomy and self-will. Men and women became the authors of their own moral law, and murder showed itself in the first family, followed by the question, "Am I my brother's keeper?" The fall was a fact, and *is* a fact. All of the vociferous arguments from Huxley and others will never quench the fire of rebellion that rages in the heart of humanity. Malcolm Muggeridge has astutely observed that the depravity of man is at once the most unpopular of all dogmas, but the most empirically verifiable. Humankind has denied God, and in that vertical rebellion begins our lostness. Society is not jeopardized as much as individuals themselves.

The Real Victim

I would like to draw two basic conclusions from this. The first is that every act of wrong, public or private, does victimize. It victimizes the one performing it and reshapes the person. Prime Minister Konoye of Japan, one of those guilty of the horrific Japanese war crimes committed during the Second World War, left by his deathbed a copy of Oscar Wilde's *De Profundis*, having carefully underlined the words, "Terrible as what the world did to me, what I did to myself was far more terrible still."[10]

I remember one occasion when a businessman, looking back on his life, shared with me his memories of a life morally mangled. He said, "It started with my imagination that reinforced certain wrong desires. Then, having made repeated choices that were clearly wrong, in betrayal after betrayal I convinced myself that what I had indulged in I needed. The more I convinced myself that I needed it, I soon redefined who I was as a person. Now, as I look at what I have become, I can no longer live with myself. I hate who I am. I am emotionally running, but I do not know where to go."

Knowing who we are and what we need is the starting point of what we will become. Until we understand what the Bible means by *sin*, our moral definitions will never find solutions. Words and platitudes in themselves have no power to change. Let us never forget that the men who sat enthralled before the strains of Wagner's music were the same men who built the death camps of Auschwitz and Birkenau. The problem is not the absence of education or culture; it is the presence of sin.

The playwright Bernard Shaw (known popularly as the author of *Pygmalion*) said:

> The first prison I ever saw had inscribed over it "Cease to do evil, learn to do well": but as the inscription was on the outside, the prisoners could not read it. It should have been addressed to the self-righteous free spectator in the street, and should have run, "All have sinned and fallen short of the glory of God."[11]

This is precisely the biblical starting point for moral rectitude: the recognition that the heart of every person is sinful, and that this predicament is spiritual, as revealed in his determination to absolute autonomy.

The second conclusion that I want to draw from our rebellion toward God is that people constantly fail to understand what sin is. They mock and attack the idea of sin as a hangover from pre-scientific beliefs. At the most, they recognize it in war crimes, or in social injustices, but somehow fail to interpret it in their own lives, personally. The most definitive illustration of the failure to understand the personalization process is in the idea contained within the following story, humorous in its detail, but painfully real in spiritual terms.

It is the story of two brothers who were rather notoriously immoral. They were synonymous with the vice that had overtaken their city. When one of them very suddenly died, the surviving brother went to the local pastor and asked him to perform the burial service. He offered him an enormous sum of money if, in his eulogy, he would refer to his deceased brother as a saint. After much pondering, the pastor agreed. As the funeral service came to an end, the pastor (in the thick of his description of the departed individual) said, "The man we have come to bury was a thief. In fact, he deserves every vile description the mind can muster. He was depraved, immoral, profligate, lewd, obscene, hateful, vicious, licentious, and the scum of the earth. But compared to his brother, he was a saint!"

The pastor may not have received the promised gift, but he certainly got across a vital point. The most deceptive aspect of our sinfulness is the pervasive tendency to self-justification by comparison to some other person. An arbitrary hierarchy of vices is set up, and we exonerate ourselves by how far up the scale we are from the bottom. Those who recognize the nature of sin understand that what renders someone a sinner is not the scale of human wickedness but the very nature and character of God. It is God's purity that we stand before, not a fluctuating moral code that varies from one society to another. When sin is understood, a moral discussion can begin—for each one of us stands accountable before God. An accountability that high makes the moral law of any land secondary to the moral law of God. Honesty and virtue are embraced because our motivation is to honor God and not merely to appear right before others.

A certain professor understood this well when he asked the members of his class to sit one seat apart during the examination in order to avoid all appearances of evil, "as the Good Book says." "What if we don't believe in the Good Book?" asked one student. "Then you put two seats between!"

An outstanding example of a higher accountability is shown to us in the life of the Old Testament patriarch Joseph. You may recall that when Potiphar's wife repeatedly tried to seduce him he answered, "I cannot do this for it would violate the trust of your husband, and break the law of God" (see Gen. 39:8–10). Joseph protected himself well, for just in case the answer was forthcoming that it would not bother the husband, there was still the law of God. Joseph saw morality through God's eyes.

Steve Turner, an English journalist, contrasted this view of morality with that of the naturalist. He said:

> If chance be
> the Father of all flesh,

disaster is his rainbow in the sky,
and when you hear
"State of emergency!"
"Sniper kills Ten!"
"Troops on Rampage!"
"Youths go Looting!"
"Bomb blasts School!"—

It is but the sound of man
worshipping his maker.

Conversely, upholding the moral law as an expression of one's love, in response to the love of God, is the sound of the Christian worshipping his or her Maker. The moral law, then, is not seen as an imposition upon the Christian from without; rather, it is a commitment born out of gratitude to the God whose love one has experienced. This relationship, undergirded and motivated by love in recognition of who God is, forms the foundation of right and wrong.

Healing from Within

Now we can understand what purpose morality serves in the Christian's life. One's moral behavior in society is an outworking of a spiritual recognition of who God is and of how one stands in God's sight. Social ethics, therefore, is always secondary to personal piety and flows from it.

The atheist starts from social ethics and is never able to anchor morality or its purpose. That starting point is in complete contradiction to the biblical understanding because when man is spiritually dislodged, his reason is estranged from the source of light and he is led into a delirium of vanity. Impiety is the precursor of immorality. To hark back to the earlier analogy by C. S. Lewis, the Christian defines why the ships are in the sea in the first place, which helps him determine how to keep them from bumping into each other. This primary and secondary role, always in that order, is underscored by Reinhold Niebuhr in *Moral Man and Immoral Society*:

Pure religious idealism does not concern itself with the social problem. It does not give itself the illusion that material and mundane advantages can be gained by the refusal to assert your claims to them. . . . Jesus did not counsel his disciples to forgive seventy times seven in order that they might convert their enemies, or make them more favorably disposed. He counseled it as an effort to approximate complete moral perfection, the perfection of God. He did not ask his followers to go the second mile in the hope that those who had impressed them into service would relent and give them freedom. He did not say that the enemy ought to be loved so that he would cease to be an enemy. He did not dwell upon the consequences of these moral actions, *because he viewed them from an inner and transcendent perspective* [italics mine] . . . The paradox of the moral life consists in this: that the highest mutuality is achieved where mutual advantages are not consciously sought as the fruit of love. For love is purest where it desires no returns for itself; and it is most potent where it is purest. Complete mutuality, with its advantages to each party to the relationship, is therefore most perfectly realized where it is not intended, but love is poured out without seeking returns. That is how the madness of religious morality, with its trans-social ideal, becomes the wisdom which achieves wholesome social consequences. For the same reason, a purely prudential morality must be satisfied with something less than the best.[12]

Although social consequences are not considered the primary purpose of morality, it would be shortsighted to deny the beneficial consequences that come from a biblical morality. Spiritual power may be different to brute power, but it certainly has its own way of conquering. To wit, the well-known social critic Dennis Prager, debating the Oxford atheistic philosopher Jonathan Glover, raised this thorny question:

"If you, Professor Glover, were stranded at the midnight hour in a desolate Los Angeles street and if, as you stepped out of your car with fear and trembling, you were suddenly to hear the weight of pounding footsteps behind you, and you saw ten burly young men who had just stepped out of a dwelling coming toward you, would it or would it not make a difference to you to know that they were coming from a Bible study?"[13]

Amidst hilarious laughter in the auditorium, Glover conceded that it would make a difference. Of course it makes a difference, because there is a logical connection.

3. The Intimations of Meaning

The question, then, arises how a spiritually estranged individual finds meaning in life by recognizing a loving Creator and a moral law. That question troubles the minds of honest skeptics because they long for the answer. Scores of books have been written on the subject of meaning. But often the academic world is seemingly unable to come to grips with reality without making it pedantic and bookish. The dry and sterile approach of obscure academic language can lose the simplicity and sublimity of life's most precious indicators. For life's realities also appear in nonacademic garb that is often recognized by the illiterate person while eluding the scholar. This is so because the clues do not always come through the pen of the latest inventive genius; conversely, often from the most simple experiences we learn the most significant truths.

A Precious Indicator

I received a powerful clue to this in my own life years ago when my daughter was less than a year old. I had been traveling for several weeks and had just returned home. As I stepped into the kitchen, I saw my little girl standing in her walker at the other end of the room, and she fastened her gaze upon me with singular attention. In all her childlike shyness she showed the longing within her own heart but was unsure of what move to make. Suddenly, she burst forth in my direction, stumbling over her own feet, and shot her arms into the air to be picked up. I lifted her out of her walker, and she wrapped her arms around me and nestled her head on my shoulder, where she stayed almost motionless for several minutes.

In those few moments, the sense of fulfillment in my being transcended any response that could be described in words, yet the feeling is well understood by parents—educated or otherwise. I did not need the erudition or cynicism of Bertrand Russell to enjoy it or repudiate it.

> A warmth within the breast could melt
> The freezing reason's colder part,
> And like a man in wrath the heart
> Stood up and answer'd "I have felt."[14]

In the case of my child, of course, the warmth within my breast was not born of wrath, but a sense of belonging, and of love's commitment. It was the touch of reality felt in my spirit.

Herein is a significant indicator for seekers of meaning—it is found in relationships. This extraordinary need and expression of humankind is reinforced again and again. An examination of life's varied situations brings us back repeatedly to the underlying craving for a relationship of love and integrity. On a few occasions I have had the privilege of visiting a prison and speaking to those who were behind bars for a variety of crimes. Repeatedly, I have heard it said unblushingly, "Please give my mom a call (or wife, brother, or sister) and tell her I miss her." On more than one occasion, when I visited a military hospital in war-torn countries or prisons within that context, the message was the same: "Tell my family I love them."

This is not proving a point from the overcharged moments of life; it is descriptive of life itself. Lee Iacocca's words in his book *Talking Straight* are very poignant:

> As I start the twilight years of my life, I still try to look back and figure out what it was all about. I'm still not sure what is meant by good fortune and success. I know fame and power are for the birds. But then life suddenly comes into focus. And, ah, there stand my kids. I love them.[15]

The thrill of relationships brings all of life into a focused expression. Human beings can relate to the material world and to the world of knowledge and machines only up to a point. If we do not rise above that, every association in our lives is reduced to that level and becomes an object for our own purposes. An inversion of the worst order then takes place. In God's economy, we are meant to love people and use things, but naturalism reverses the order.

Leo Tolstoy revealed in *My Confession* that the blatant blunder of his own life was the love of writing and of human acclaim, which robbed him of the treasured relationships that bring meaning.

If relationships bring meaning to life, then the ultimate mockery

> *If relationships bring meaning to life, then the ultimate mockery of life is the reality that all relationships are either ruptured by sin or severed by death.*

of life is the reality that all relationships are either ruptured by sin or severed by death. Each of us longs for a relationship that cannot be victimized by sin or destroyed by death. That relationship can only be found with God. Once that relationship is established, it serves as a blueprint for all other relationships, bringing the strength of genuine love and shunning the cancer of selfishness.

A Unified Purpose

Let us probe a little deeper. It is not sufficient to deal with the concept of meaning in only one context. Let me attempt, then, to unwrap the package of that concept in Christian terms. There are at least three areas in which meaning in life for the Christian brings cohesiveness and keeps life from becoming fragmented. These are the individual and oneself, the individual with one's community, and the individual with history. When these areas are understood and kept in balance, internally, externally, and in relation to time, then all of life becomes meaningful.

Let us consider the first area of internal integration—the individual and oneself. The Christian does not capitulate to one faculty exclusively. He or she does not see a human life as all brain or all emotion. Rather, one sees oneself endowed with the image of God and an integration of different capacities. This means that one's individuality, when lived out within the moral boundaries of a loving relationship with God, brings a total fulfillment through a diversity of expressions, converging in the purpose of one's creation. The rational, the aesthetic, the emotional, the pragmatic—all work together for good. The examined life truly becomes worth living. One's conscience responds to the holiness of God; one's mind is nurtured and nourished by the truth of God; one's imagination is enlarged and purified by the beauty of God; one's heart, or impulses, responds to the love of God; one's will surrenders to the purpose of God.

For this very reason Jesus said, "If anyone would come after me, he must deny himself and take up his cross daily and follow me" (Luke 9:23). The whole point of this challenge is to die to one's own self-centered pursuits and to build one's entire life with God's honor as the primary motivation.

Does this mean a stifling of the individual? Absolutely not. This is precisely what C. S. Lewis meant when he used the expression, "His compulsion our freedom." An incisive definition of such freedom comes to us from the pen of Rudolph Bultmann, professor of New Testament at Marburg University from 1921–1951:

> Genuine freedom is not subjective arbitrariness, but freedom from the motivation of the moment. . . . Freedom is obedience to a law of which the validity is recognized and accepted, which man recognizes as the law of his own being.[16]

The atheist, recognizing no law of his own being other than survival, finds himself a constant slave of the moment. One may then walk down a slippery slope into further bondage and self-defacement, finally to become a number, imprisoned by the self-gratifying desires of others.

Every demand of Bultmann's definition of freedom is met by the Christian belief. A Christian is not a slave to momentary values that are selectively applied, but obedient to a law, the validity of which he recognizes as the law of one's own being. He is rescued from both pragmatism and alienation—the former being shortsighted and the latter leading to despair. Life is viewed not just in its constituent and isolated parts, but in its cohesive and purposive whole. The internal cohesion that God brings makes for psychological well-being. Contrary to Sigmund Freud, true spirituality, properly understood, is not an obsession or escape; rather, it rescues us from obsessions that do not satisfy and which, in turn, force us to escape via drugs or otherwise.[17]

The Christian perspective bridges the gap between theory and practice. A total submission of life to a higher law is brought to bear upon every decision. The mind-set is not impulsive or reactionary, but acts according to a purpose affirmed in advance. The Christian's enjoyment of this God-given freedom brings both unity and continuity. One cannot compartmentalize one's private and public lives without destroying purpose. One cannot do in private what vitiates the very purpose of one's life. The Christian's freedom is not in the liberty to do what one wants, but in finding the strength in God to do what one should.

Jesus said, "The thief comes only to steal and kill and destroy; I have come that they may have life, and have it to the full" (John 10:10). Jesus was saying exactly the opposite of what the Christian life has often been portrayed to be. By his detractors, Christ is seen as the robber of human endeavor and the roadblock to our fanciful flights of pleasure, an expectation that Francis Thompson struggled with in "The Hound of Heaven":

> I fled Him, down the nights and down the days;
> I fled Him, down the arches of the years;
> I fled Him, down the labyrinthine ways
>   Of my own mind; and in the mist of tears
> I hid from Him, and under running laughter. . . .
>
> (For, though I knew His love Who followèd,
>   Yet was I sore adread
> Lest, having Him, I must have naught beside.)[18]

But true liberation, contrary to the expectations of many, is found by surrender to him. Unfortunately for Thompson, before he saw the contrariness of his fear, his life had been marred and robbed by opium. Even so, he clearly concluded that it was in Christ that life's ultimate problem of unity and diversity could be solved. He himself had to be unified within, and he could not do this apart from Christ.

So liberating is this internal work of Christ that it can only be described as a new birth. The songwriter said:

> Heaven above is softer blue,
> Earth around is sweeter green,
> Something lives in every hue
> Christless eyes have never seen.[19]

This transformation of vision, bordering on mystery, is the work of Christ within the heart of human beings. This is the spiritual birth Christ talks about that opens one's eyes to see this world as God sees it and to understand oneself for the first time. The work of Christ in regenerating the human heart brings the beginning of meaning and understanding. Unless a person starts here, he or she is lost.

> We shall not cease from exploration,
> And the end of all our exploring
> Will be to arrive where we started
> And know the place for the first time.[20]

Malcolm Muggeridge expressed this glorious triumph of surrender when he realized what had happened within him. Here is a man, who as a peripatetic journalist, had covered the globe. He had rubbed shoulders with the newsmakers of the day but concluded that all news is old news happening to new people. The best news for him was the good news of the gospel, with the new birth for an old heart that had lost so much in the most energetic years of his life. In his book *Jesus Rediscovered* (which someone has said would be more aptly titled *Muggeridge Rediscovered*), he said:

I may, I suppose, regard myself as a relatively successful man. People occasionally stare at me in the streets; that's fame. I can fairly easily earn enough to qualify for admission to the higher slopes of the Internal Revenue Service. That's success. Furnished with money and a little fame, even the elderly, if they care to, may partake of trendy diversions. That's pleasure. It might happen once in awhile that something I said or wrote was sufficiently heeded for me to persuade myself that it represented a serious impact on our time—that's fulfillment. Yet, I say to you,—and beg you to believe me,—multiply these tiny triumphs by millions, add them all together, and they are nothing,—less than nothing, a positive impediment—measured against one drop of that living water Christ offers to the spiritually thirsty, irrespective of who or what they are.[21]

Christ brings meaning by harnessing us in our innermost being, and rescues us from being fragmented within. Thomas Merton summed up a volume of theology in one statement: "Man is not at peace with his fellow man because he is not at peace with himself; he is not at peace with himself, because he is not at peace with God."[22]

A Personal Significance

The second way Christ brings meaning is by retaining the worth of the individual without losing the value of the community at large. The tension of individual freedom vis-à-vis societal good is countered by a different vantage point. The Bible says, "For God so loved the world that he gave his one and only Son, that whoever believes in him shall not perish but have eternal life" (John 3:16). God's love for the world is portrayed, but the application is individual. He does not spend his love in the generalities of a mass appeal but rather in the particularities of each individual.

History reminds us of a politician who had taken up the cause of a minority group. So engrossed had he become in defending the rights of this victimized segment of society that every endeavor he made was to that end. From slogans, to speeches, to laws, this passion had enveloped his life. One day, shortly before he was to deliver a pivotal speech on the subject, a teenager from the minority group came to ask for a moment of his time. Instead of responding to this specific request, he looked at his assistant and said, "Tell that man that since I have taken up his cause I have no time left for the individual." The assistant paused and said, "That is incredible, Sir! Even God has not reached that stage, yet."

In the demands of life upon us we often find ourselves devalued or diminished, if not completely effaced, in the face of mass society. The yearning for value, and the wish to keep life personally important so that it is not drowned in a sea of causes, is accomplished by God alone.

It is this very balance that is seen time and time again in the life of Jesus. He had compassion on the masses: he was concerned for the crowd that had no food; he was incensed at the religious exploitation of people at the hands of the temple demagogues; and he wept over a city that brought anguish to his prophetic soul, for he saw them as sheep without a shepherd. And to the same city to which he had said, "Oh Jerusalem! How often would I have gathered you," he demonstrated the value of every individual. He did not miss the cry of the beggar, the halting plea of the lame person, and the emptiness of the rich man or the educated Pharisee. He told the parable of the shepherd who left the ninety-nine sheep to look for the one who had wandered away and was lost. The parables of the lost coin and the lost son underscore that he came to seek and save those which are lost—and that all have sinned and fallen short of the standard of God.

My son once played Tee Ball. The boys were so small, and their headgear so big, that in order to see anything their heads were constantly tilted in an apparent examination of the sky. In short, nothing fit because they were so diminutive. Thankfully, the ball was set on a tee so that they could contort their bodies into a posture from which they could get a glimpse of the motionless ball. With the number of options they were given, every player, sooner or later, connected. And I noticed something. Every time my son hit that ball and arrived safely on base, the first thing he did was to look in my direction to see if I was watching. Yes, they all played to the crowd. And yes, it was a team effort. But amid the sounds of the spectators and the backslapping of the teammates, there was always the need for, "Did you see me do that, Dad?"

One's most personal need cannot be lost and traded in the abstraction of a faceless and nameless crowd. For the Christian, meaning comes in upholding the value of the individual, who is not subsumed under the category of "people." At the same time, society is not made indeterminate, so as to make individual needs exclusive of society's. God's process for bringing about change in society has always been through the hearts of men and women; bringing about change from within, rather than making short-term

> *God's process for bringing about change in society has always been through the hearts of men and women; bringing about change from within, rather than making short-term gains by mere legislation from without.*

gains by mere legislation from without. A Christian in society is like salt to water—society can never absorb one without being changed itself.

From an internal coalescing of the diversities within each individual, to the distinctive value of the individual in society, the Christian message breathes meaning into life.

A Transcending Motivation

This brings me to the vital role of the individual as he or she relates to time in general and to history in particular. The Christian faith stands in a unique position here, as it addresses the flow of history through the heartbeat of individual lives. To understand this, we must try to comprehend the way this relationship is viewed in contrary philosophies.

From the Christian perspective we see the finger of God in all of history, and Christ as its central figure. The Christian explains history through the eternal eyes of Christ.

By contrast, the traditionalist lives for the past; the existentialist lives for the now; and the futurist or utopianist lives for the future.

Notice the words of Jesus Christ as he broke bread with the disciples, "For whenever you eat this bread and drink this cup [emphasis on the present], you proclaim the Lord's death [a look to the past], until he comes [the anticipation of the future]" (1 Cor. 11:26). For the Christian, the present stands on the shoulders of the past in anticipation of the future, fusing every moment with significance. Everything matters—even a million years from now. There is nothing that escapes the sharp knife-edge of importance and reality.

The life of the Scotsman Eric Liddell, who was a devout Christian and a superb athlete, was featured in contradistinction to Harold Abrams in the film *Chariots of Fire*. Abrams, we recall, underscored his emptiness by finding even winning to be anticlimactic. Liddell's life, and his striving for excellence, was an expression of his love for God—everything mattered because his life was committed to Christ. The lines in the film that capture this best are uttered by Liddell to his sister: "Jenny, God has made me for a purpose—for China; but he has also made me fast, and when I run, I feel his pleasure."

Liddell won the 400 meters gold medal in the 1924 Olympics and later became a missionary to China, where he died. His enjoyment of God in every endeavor and service for Christ was a strong reminder that nothing for the Christian is essentially secular. It can only be secularized by leaving God out of it or by engaging in that from which God, by his nature, must be excluded.

4. Destined for Life

The lines are now clearly drawn. The naturalist has no intelligent cause to look to, no moral law to point to, no essential meaning to cling to, and finally, no hope to look forward to for one's destiny.

For the Christian, the resurrection of Christ from the dead is the tour de force of one's apologetic and guarantees one's destiny. The resurrection is the linchpin of one's argument as he or she defends the Christian faith. It addresses the most painful of all of life's struggles—the agony of death, which cuts us all down and taunts any hankering we have for omniscience.

So vital to the nerve and sinew of the Gospel narrative is the issue of life after death that the cumulative force of Christ's early

life and teaching is suddenly forgotten by his disciples, who are left
in a state of deep puzzlement after the crucifixion. After his death
the disciples, who had abandoned everything and followed him,
hovered between a sense of despondency and a sense of betrayal.

They had placed all their hopes and ambitions in the claims of
Jesus that he was the Son of God and would fulfill all their messianic
expectations. Now the dream had been shattered. The summation of
all their responses began with the words, "We had hoped. . . ."

It was the encounter with the risen Christ that finally transformed
the band of disciples.

No longer hiding behind closed doors in the grip of intellectual
ridicule, they became the most influential people of their time—
until even Rome, with all her pompous power, was conquered
by the Christian message. Every endeavor to obliterate this message, through threat of persecution to the force of extermination,
failed.

As Chesterton said, "Christianity has died many times and risen
again; for it has a God who knows the way out of the grave."

With the message of Christ, anchored in his resurrection, the
words of twentieth-century historian Will Durant are justified:
"Caesar and Christ had met in the arena, and Christ had won."[23]

The Only Hope

Without question, it was the conquered grave that gave the message its impetus. The man who best exemplified this radical change
was Saul of Tarsus, known to the world as the apostle Paul. This
young man was a Hebrew by birth, who had studied at the feet of
Gamaliel. He was a citizen of Rome, the central city of the great
empire to which all roads led, the center of pagan culture. He was
raised in the Greek city of Tarsus, whose university eclipsed even
that of Athens. His background could not have been better suited
to speak to the world. The Hebrews gave the world its moral categories; the Greeks its philosophical categories; and the Romans
its legal categories. With prerogatives of birth and privileges of
learning, young Saul was the immovable object that could not
be dislodged, except by the irresistible force—the person of Jesus

Christ. That occurred in the spectacular postresurrection encounter on the Damascus road.

So dramatic and persuasive was this confrontation, that it became, for Paul, the most incontestable authentication of who Jesus was. He was repeatedly brought before questioning authorities, because they knew of the potency of a firsthand testimony from a man such as this. Before the Sanhedrin, he began his defense with the words, "My brothers, I am a Pharisee, the son of a Pharisee. I stand on trial because of my hope in the resurrection of the dead. . . ." Before King Agrippa and Festus he concluded his witness by saying, "What I am saying is true and reasonable. The king is familiar with these things, and I can speak freely to him. I am convinced that none of this has escaped his notice, because it was not done in a corner." In front of a vast crowd, in the meeting of the Areopagus in Athens, he climaxed his apologetic for the Christian faith with the fact of the resurrection.

It all seems so simplistic, does it not? A group of gullible, prescientific men, succumbing to the illusions and deceptions of their day. Yet, every piece of evidence mustered, including the prophesies that long preceded the event itself and the unexplainable change in the courage and confidence of the early believers, supported by the empirical evidence, argues powerfully for the truth of it all. The Jewish and Roman authorities needed to do only one thing to have smothered this belief and rendered it a farce. All they needed to do was to produce the body of Christ—but they could not. Paul himself granted that, had the resurrection not taken place, Christians were of all men to be most pitied.[24]

Paul was too much of a thinker to construct his life on an uncertain foundation of credulity. He shunned all deductions that were established on false premises. Yet, this persecutor of the early church, who had called for the death penalty for those "seduced" by the Christian message, found himself a trailblazer for the cause of Christ.

It was the knowledge and conviction that Christ had truly broken the chains of death and conquered the grave that gave Paul his hope. It impelled him from within and became the compelling and enduring feature of his proclamation. He feared no man or power because he knew him, whom to know is life eternal. Paul stood in a unique position to the other disciples. They all knew Jesus in the chronological sequence of his birth, life, death, and resurrection. Paul encountered him in the logical sequence of his resurrection, death, life, and birth. Through the keyhole of the resurrection, he argued backwards in time; for through it he saw the authentication of Christ's message, the explanation of his death, the meaning of his life, and the prophetic fulfillment of his birth. These coalesced to make Christ the centerpiece of history. God indeed had spoken and the authenticity of his message was demonstrated with his power over death.

The whole landscape of life now lay before Paul, interpreted through the eyes of the risen Christ. The empirically verifiable fact of the resurrection became the peg on which he hung his whole destiny. It is, and has been, the resurrection that has brought hope to the hearts and minds of people across the centuries.

Dr. Billy Graham told of an occasion when German Chancellor Konrad Adenauer was in conversation with him. Mr. Adenauer asked Dr. Graham, "Do you believe in the resurrection of Jesus Christ from the dead?" When Dr. Graham immediately answered that indeed he did, there was a long silence from the Chancellor, and then he said, "Outside of the resurrection of Jesus Christ, I know of no other hope for mankind."

That is an extraordinary and yet most meaningful statement, made by one of the great statesmen of the twentieth century. It is highly significant because it spoke volumes, coming from a man who had to pick up the ruins after Hitler had left the world mangled.

The Paradigm Shift

C. S. Lewis, addressing this same theme in an allegorical form that appeals to all ages, effectively captures this powerful truth in his book *The Lion, the Witch and the Wardrobe*. The Lion, Aslan, is a symbol of Christ in his majestic, yet gentle power. The Witch represents the Devil. Young Edmund has sold out to the Witch through the enticement of the Turkish delight she offered him. His yielding to this allurement would entail the betrayal of Aslan and his brother and sisters. Implicit in the choice was the grasping of autonomy and a deliberate abandonment of the will and counsel of Aslan. Unknown to Edmund, the penalty exacted for this treacherous act is his own death, as encoded within the laws of the "deep magic." Because of his unquenchable love for Edmund, now mingled with grief, Aslan has offered to die in his place and bear the full force of his penalty. The Witch is ecstatic, for the destruction of Aslan is what she had really sought. Only then could she rule Narnia, unhindered by Aslan's influence. Aslan is placed, battered and bound, on the ceremonial Stone Table. The children are dismayed as they witness his humiliation and death, and the silence that ensues is punctuated by the sobs of their disappointment and grief.

Yet suddenly, there is the unmistakable sound of the cracking of the Stone Table; and as the bewildered children hasten back to the scene, they are greeted by Aslan, triumphant over his death. Unable to comprehend the immensity of this event, the children yearn for an explanation.

> "It means," said Aslan, "that though the Witch knew the Deep Magic, there is a magic deeper still which she did not know. Her knowledge only goes back to the dawn of Time. But if she could have looked a little further back, into the stillness and the darkness before Time dawned, she would have read there a different incantation. She would have known that when a willing victim who had committed no treachery was killed in a traitor's stead, the Table would crack and Death itself would start working backwards."[25]

C. S. Lewis, who was a master of imagery, captured profound biblical truths in this simple story. He provided a glimpse of life's realities from the vantage point of the author of life, whom death could not contain. The cracking of the Table and Death working backwards are symbolic and figurative expressions of the actual redefinitions of life itself. Kierkegaard expressed the same idea when he spoke of defining life backwards and living it forwards: starting from his destiny and redefining the journey. This destiny that we can know helps us alter our whole direction in life. It makes sense, for every journey must begin by knowing the destiny. The poem quoted earlier, "Seven Are We," has an interesting history. Wordsworth said that in writing that poem, with the help of Coleridge, he started by writing the last verse first. This is truly instructive for life itself, for if one does not know where he is going, is it any wonder that he does not know that he is lost?

This is the ultimate paradigm shift; life does not end at the grave. Now, through the eyes of him who conquered death, there is hope

> *This is the ultimate paradigm shift;*
> *life does not end at the grave.*
> *Now, through the eyes of him who conquered*
> *death, there is hope for humankind, and all*
> *of life's essentials are redefined.*

for humankind, and all of life's essentials are redefined. G. K. Chesterton captured this idea so well in his poem on the raising of Lazarus from the dead. Putting words into the mouth of this one who had just emerged from the tomb, he said:

> After one moment, when I bowed my head
> And the whole world turned over and came upright,
> And I walked out where the old road shone white,
> I walked the ways and heard what all men said, . . .
>
> The sages have a hundred maps to give
> That tract their crawling cosmos like a tree,
> They rattle reason out through many a sieve
> That stores the dust and lets the gold go free:
> And all these things are less than dust to me
> Because my name is Lazarus, and I live.[26]

Paul W. Hoon has written:

Jesus Christ continually contradicts us in the way we experience ourselves as alive, and compels us to radically redefine what we mean by life. He encounters us the way he encountered the disciples on Easter Sunday. They were the ones marked out for death. Those who survived him were really the "dead." He the "dead" one was really the living.[27]

Job's question, "If a man die, shall he live again?" is resoundingly answered. Our destiny is explained, and the way we view life must be altered.

The Truth Comes Home

When my own mother passed away, the one thought in my mind was the word, "Gone." The more I pondered it, the more it sounded forth—"Gone, gone, gone." As I came to grips with the promise of Christ, made to those who have made that commitment to him as their Lord and Savior, I felt the thought completed. Jesus said to Martha by the grave of her brother Lazarus, "I am the resurrection and the life." Elsewhere he said to the disciples, "Because I live, you also will live." My mother had not just gone, she had gone home to be with her Lord. She had served him with her heart and mind. There is an eternal difference between being "gone" and having "gone home."

This is the hope of which the Christian lyricist Don Wyrtzen wrote:

> When engulfed by the terror of tempestuous sea
> Unknown waves before you roll
> At the end of doubt and peril is eternity
> Though fear and conflict seize your soul
>
> When surrounded by the blackness of the darkest night
> Oh how lonely death can be
> At the end of this long tunnel is a shining light
> For death is swallowed up in victory
>
> But just think of stepping on shore
>   and finding it heaven
> Of touching a hand and finding it God's
> Of breathing new air and finding it celestial
> Of waking up in glory and finding it home[28]

This song only echoes what Paul had said in his letter to the Corinthians:

> Behold, I [show] you a mystery: we shall not all sleep, but we shall all be changed. In a moment, in the twinkling of an eye, at the last trump: for the trumpet shall sound, and the dead shall be raised in-corruptible, and we shall be changed. For this corruptible must put on incorruption, and this mortal must put on immortality. So when this corruptible shall have put on incorruption, and this mortal shall have put on immortality, then shall be brought to pass the saying that is written, "Death is swallowed up in victory." O death, where is your sting? O grave, where is your victory?
>
> 1 Corinthians 15:51–55 KJV

In recognizing the power of Christ over the grave, we are able to see, in this tightly-knit universe in which we live, a wonderful design, morality, meaning, and hope.

The Final Analysis

I have attempted to sustain the major assertions of the Christian in a threefold approach. (Appendix 1 goes into detail on the nature and necessity of this.) The composite nature of human beings and the cohesive nature of truth demand such criteria. Applying this to the resurrection, we have seen the empirically verifiable argument presented by the disciples; C. S. Lewis beautifully capturing the nobility of the imagination in illustrating this truth in *The Lion, the Witch and the Wardrobe*; and the power of these truths being applied in the death of a loved one. The argument, the illustration, and the application bring wisdom to the mind, hope for the heart, and guidance in life.

By contrast, this same approach in carefully scrutinizing athe-ism shows the weakness of its defense and the immensity of its loss—even greater than Nietzsche imagined. I have sought to touch on just four areas of loss—the leaps of ignorance into primal causa-tion; the loss of morality; the absence of meaning; and the death of hope. These result in a fragmentation, giving rise to answers that cannot be consistent when explaining our origin, condition, salvation, and destiny.

But that is not all that is lost for the atheist. One other aspect must be stated: if the atheist is wrong, there is no recovery of that which he has lost. This was precisely Pascal's wager:

> Yes; but you must wager. It is not optional. You are embarked. Which will you choose then? Let us see. Since you must choose, let us see which interests you least. You have two things to lose, the true and the good; and two things to stake, your reason and your will, your knowledge and your happiness; and your nature has two things to shun, error and misery. Your reason is no more shocked in choosing one rather than the other, since you must of necessity choose. This is one point settled. But your happiness? Let us weigh the gain and the loss in wagering that God is. Let us estimate these two chances. If you gain, you gain all; if you lose, you lose nothing. Wager, then, without hesitation that He is.[29]

Pascal's argument should never be offered as a proof for God's existence or as a reason for belief in him. This was never Pascal's intention. Such an argument would be flawed by using experience as a starting point and could end up holding a fragile faith tied to an even more fragile reason. This wager is not to be dismissed as a fatalistic plunge, taken when reason has caved in. Rather, as Pascal argued, he attempted to meet only one challenge of atheism, and that is the test of existential self-fulfillment. Atheism, therefore, could not justifiably argue against his experience, if experience were all that mattered. In fact, Pascal said that he had more than mere self-fulfillment. He had everything the Christian faith promised to him, including the climactic hope beyond the grave. Should, however, death be the end, he did not sense any loss, for contentment in life was still his. That is all he was saying.

The atheist, on the other hand, having rejected God, flutters between pleasurable options, with inner peace forever eluding him. If, after death, he should find out that there is a God, his loss has been irreparable; for not only did contentment and peace elude him in this life, but death has opened the door to an ultimate and eternal lostness. All judgments bring with them a margin of error. But no judgment ought to carry with it the potential for so irretrievable a loss that every possible gain is unworthy of merit. The atheist makes precisely such a hazardous judgment. It is an all-or-nothing gamble

> *The atheist risks everything for the present and the future, on the basis of a belief that we are uncaused by any intelligent being. We just happen to be here. That one is willing to live and die in that belief is a very high price to pay for conjecture.*

of self, thrust into the slot machine of life. It is a faith beyond the scope of reason.

The atheist risks everything for the present and the future, on the basis of a belief that we are uncaused by any intelligent being. We just happen to be here. That one is willing to live and die in that belief is a very high price to pay for conjecture.

5. The Privilege or Peril of Choice

The difference and the choice become crystal clear: either a person yields his heart and will to the rulership of God or he chooses to retain complete autonomy, irrespective of the consequences. God has revealed himself in this world and in his Word. We see within ourselves a battlefield: there is that within us that tugs toward autonomy and manifests our depravity and that within us that points us to God, in whose image we were made. Each must choose, for to live with the contradiction tears one apart. The words of Pascal are graphic:

> What a chimera then is man! what a novelty, what a monster, what a chaos, what a subject of contradiction, what a prodigy! A judge of

all things, feeble worm of the earth, depository of the truth; cloaca of uncertainty and error, the glory and the shame of the universe.[30]

In choosing between one's options, a person's essential dignity and ultimate destiny are at stake. In the atheist's case, he pursues a self-indulgent glory, which ends up in shame. The Christian, recognizing his shame before God, is spiritually transformed to see the glory for which each of us was created. Herein is the point at which every atheist has to face up to with unadulterated honesty: It is only as one recognizes the poverty of one's spirit that one finds the joyful surprise of a life enriched by God a thousandfold.

An unforgettable illustration is found in the burial of Empress Zita, the last Hapsburg Empress. Thousands fell in line behind the catafalque, drawn by six black horses. The procession came to a stop at the Capuchin Church, and there, a long-observed tradition was enacted. As a member of the funeral party knocked on the closed door of the church, a voice from within asked, "Who goes there?"

The titles were read aloud: "Queen of Bohemia, Dalmatia, Croatia, Slavonia, Galicia. Queen of Jerusalem, Grand Duchess of Tuscany and Krakow."

"I do not know her," came the response from within the church.

A second knock, and the question of "Who goes there?" brought forth the response, "Zita, Empress of Austria and Queen of Hungary."

Again the reply, "I do not know her."

When the inevitable question was put the third time, the answer was simply, "Zita, a sinning mortal." "Come in," came the welcoming voice, as the doors were slowly opened.

The atheist's biggest struggle comes here. A man or woman rejects God neither because of intellectual demands nor because of the paucity of evidence. One rejects God because of a moral resistance that refuses to admit one's need for God. God invites each one to come to him, the Author of life, and receive his salvation offered through Jesus Christ. Jesus himself reminds us that it will profit a man nothing if he gains the whole world and loses his own soul. But to the one who trusts in him, he offers life in all its fullness. Jesus said:

> Is not life more important than food, and the body more important than clothes? . . . See how the lilies of the field grow. They do not labor or spin. Yet I tell you, not even Solomon in all his splendor was dressed like one of these. If that is how God clothes the grass of the field, which is here today, and tomorrow is thrown into the fire, will he not much more clothe you, O you of little faith? So do not worry, saying, "What shall we eat?" or "What shall we drink?" or "What shall we wear?" For the pagans run after all these things, and your heavenly Father knows that you need them. But seek first his kingdom, and his righteousness, and all these things will be given to you as well.
>
> Matthew 6:25, 28–33

Our primary pursuit should be God himself, and all secondary and tertiary pursuits fall into place. It is not accidental that the last paragraph of the last book of the Bible is punctuated with the word *come*. That is God's invitation. " 'Come!' Whoever is thirsty, let him come; and whoever wishes, let him take the free gift of the water of life" (Rev. 22:17).

Questions for Study and Discussion

1. What particular apologetic argument does God use with Job in answering his charges? (See pp. 119–21.) Notice that this approach is not merely cognitive—though this particular argument is often made as purely evidential—but that God speaks to the depth of Job's heart and opens his eyes to mystery. Does this approach address some of your own deeply felt questions? How might you model this approach in your own conversations?
2. How does the Christian approach to knowledge differ from the atheist?
3. What does the author call "the second major affirmation of theism"? (See p. 125.) Discuss what ways this affirmation "is

powerfully sustained in the human experience." How does the Bible speak to this issue?

4. What are three areas in which the Christian perspective provides meaning for the individual? (See p. 138.) Comment further on these in relation to your own life.

5. The philosopher Søren Kierkegaard expressed that in order to live life well, we must define it backwards: the starting point must be our destiny. Discuss this idea and how it might alter your direction in life. How do C. S. Lewis (particularly his *The Lion, the Witch and the Wardrobe*) and Blaise Pascal similarly approach this question?

APPENDIX

I

THE FINGER OF TRUTH AND THE FIST OF REALITY

If you make people think they're thinking, they'll love you: but if you really make them think, they'll hate you.

—Don Marquis

Somebody once wrote to the English writer G. K. Chesterton and asked him what he thought about civilization. Chesterton promptly replied, "I think it is a wonderful idea, why doesn't somebody start one?"

The moral bankruptcy that stalks our land and the existential emptiness so evident in our youth today remove any temptation to brand this Chesterton response as cynical. What is harder to admit is the cause-effect relationship between atheism and our present crisis.

At first glance one may wish to dispute the allegation that atheism is the womb that conceived our moral malady. But a careful examination of its assumptions and conclusions reveals it to be a system indefensible against that charge and many others. It incorporates in its worldview several fatal flaws, making it a costly and dangerous philosophy on which to build a life or destiny.

The philosophical process I have undertaken is somewhat akin to the three-step method that leads us to any conclusion: our assumptions, our arguments, and our applications. This necessitated incursions into the realm of logic, the testing of its conclusions in experience, and the mandating of those applications as prescriptive for others. Putting it differently, I have had to cover ground from the logically persuasive (that which can be demonstrated by argument) to the experientially relevant (that which can be tested and illustrated in life). Only after these steps can one establish norms and make applications for life. When atheism is tested along these lines, its vulnerability is seen in contrast to the cohesive strength of theism.

The word *philosophy* for many spells boredom, if not grief. Philosophy is to a student's mind what spinach is to a child's taste buds—a punishment to be endured but of questionable value. The other extreme is when it becomes to the philosopher what spinach is to Popeye—the sole and sufficient means to cerebral muscle-flexing. Here it sets itself up as the supreme authority on reality, capable of decimating any enemy, and hence of ultimate value. I have endeavored to rescue the arguments from both extremes, so that we neither allow the allegation that philosophers are mere wordsmiths nor do we allow them to take unto themselves the responsibility

> *As C. S. Lewis asserted, everyone in life has a philosophy—the only question is, whether it is a good one.*

of being the ticket inspectors into heaven. As C. S. Lewis asserted, everyone in life has a philosophy—the only question is, whether it is a good one. He said, "Good philosophy must exist, if for no other reason, because bad philosophy needs to be answered."[1]

The Front Door of Reason

Philosophy, as I see it, comes to us at three levels. The first level is the foundation, the theoretical substructure upon which inductions are made and deductions are postulated. Put plainly, it depends heavily upon the form and the force of an argument. Logic, to most minds, has never overflowed with romance and has seldom triggered excitement. Ambrose Bierce, an American writer and journalist, defined it as "the art of thinking and reasoning in strict accordance with the limitations and incapacities of the human understanding."[2] Logic, unfortunately, also lends itself to the same critique Somerset Maugham made of perfection, "Perfection is a trifle dull."[3] With all of our resistance to it, however, one unavoidably must use it to test truth claims; moreover it is impossible to attack logic without using logic. For, truth has a direct bearing on reality, and the laws of logic do apply in every sphere of our lives. The classic illustration states:

> All men are mortal.
> Socrates is a man.
> Therefore, Socrates is mortal.

It is hard to argue against that, regardless of how dull it sounds.

Since the laws of logic apply to reality, it is imperative that these laws be understood if any argument is to stand its ground. This can be a vast subject in itself, but the foundational laws are indispensable to the communication of truth.

Peter Kreeft, professor of philosophy at Boston College, has briefly addressed the importance of correct argumentation in his book *Three Philosophies of Life*. In a subsection "Rules for Talking Back," he writes the following:

Three things must go right with any argument:

(1) The terms must be unambiguous
(2) The premises must be true
(3) The argument must be logical.

Conversely, three things can go wrong with any argument:

(1) The terms may be ambiguous
(2) The premises may be false
(3) The argument may be illogical.[4]

In any argument, the application of these rules cannot be compromised if the conclusion is to be defended or refuted. Truth is indispensable to each statement, and validity is indispensable to each deduction. This dual combination of truth and validity is central to the persuasiveness of any argument, and if there is a flaw in either of the two, it fails.

Many commonly held beliefs are prone to such mistakes. For example, take an often used argument that is assumed to be a proof against the existence of God.

(1) There is evil in the world.
(2) If there were a God, he would have done something about it.
(3) Nothing has been done about it.
(4) Therefore, there is no God.

Notice that the third premise is not self-evident, but instead is a deduction in itself in need of inductive support. It can be shown to fail the test of truthfulness and validity because it reveals the presuppositions of an individual. For it says nothing about whether God exists or not, but only that if he did, he would make himself more plain and do things "my way."

Despite the weakness of the third premise, this type of argument from atheists presents a logical dilemma for theists. Responding to this, theists may make several approaches as a starting point. Their goal will be to first defang the question and then present stronger arguments for God's existence.

The issue of evil is, of course, one of the greatest debating points between theism and atheism. Let me give just two meaningful approaches theists may use as starting points.

Approach 1

1. Yes, there is evil in this world.
2. If there is evil, there must be good (a problem the atheist has to explain).
3. If there is good and evil, there must be a moral law on which to judge between good and evil.

4. If there is a moral law, there must be a moral law giver.
5. For the theist, this points to God.

With this as a starting point, theists can mitigate the force of the argument from evil and then deal with underlying assumptions. They can show that some assumptions are not consistent with an atheistic worldview. Then, as a final step theists can present the arguments for God's existence and explain what God has said (and done) about the problem of evil.

Approach 2

1. There is evil in the world.
2. There is nothing inconsistent about evil and the freedom of the will within the framework of a loving Creator.
3. In fact, concepts of love and goodness are unexplainable unless there is a God.
4. Since human beings do experience love and goodness, it argues for the reality of God.
5. Therefore, it is not unreasonable to believe that God exists.

From here theists begin their arguments for the existence of God. Atheists may challenge some of these premises, but this is how the arguments and counterarguments are fashioned.

There are many excellent books written on the subject. The problem of evil has many facets that need to be dealt with—the moral problem, the physical problem, the metaphysical problem, and so on. Also, under discussion would be the issue of "the best of all possible worlds." The books *The Problem of Pain* by C. S. Lewis and *Philosophy of Religion* by Norman Geisler both contain representative discussions of the problem of evil. Lewis deals with the problem existentially, and Geisler, philosophically.

I have illustrated the foregoing to show that logic is pivotal in any discussion of God's existence. At some point everyone uses it to either challenge or defend the existence of God. Not everyone desires to delve too deeply into the laws of logic, but the reasoning process that forms an argument is used every day, by everyone, without our even being aware of it. It is just underscored more conspicuously in an issue as significant as the existence of God. This ought not to be surprising, because wherever there is an assertion of truth, the possibility is left open for a counterclaim that is false. That is why C. S. Lewis argued that good philosophy needs to exist, if for no other reason than that bad philosophy needs to be answered. The process of proper argumentation is one step toward the acceptance of truth and the rejection of error.

In any argument, therefore, if there is no accepted or demonstrable truthfulness in the premises, or if there is an invalid deduction, the argument fails. This is level one in our philosophical approach, the theoretical realm in which the laws of logic are applied to real-

> *To deny the laws of logic is futile and self-defeating because one must use reason to either sustain or challenge an argument.*

ity. To deny their application is futile and self-defeating—and then language becomes nonsensical—because again, one must use reason to either sustain or challenge an argument. In short, level one deals with *why* one believes what he or she believes and is sustained by the process of logical reasoning to guide us to the truth.

The Back Door of the Arts

The second level of philosophy does not feel the constraints of reason or come under the binding strictures of argument. It finds its refuge in *the imagination and feeling*. Ways of thinking at this level may enter one's consciousness via a play or a novel, or touch the imagination through visual media, making belief-altering impact by capturing the emotions. It is immensely effective, and literature, drama, and music have historically molded the soul of a nation far more than textbooks that plumbed the depths of language, truth, and logic. Level two is existential and may fallaciously claim that it need not bow to the laws of logic. When this second approach holds sway, some might contend that logicians deal with arid theories, but the existentialist, they argue, deals with life, sensation, and feeling.

However, this second level, or approach, has within it both strength and weakness. Its strength is that felt needs are met; its weakness is that feelings create absolutes. Unfortunately, in our day more than ever before, the imagination has been assaulted in every direction so as to invade our consciences with disturbing visions and distorting sounds of reality that shun the constructive and uplift the bizarre and violent. Consequently, emotions are manipulated that produce dissonance in life rather than harmony. For the imagination may be turned into fancy, and rather than serving the cause of beauty or good, may become an avenue of strife and evil. Therein lies its danger. An abused imagination yields perversions that defy reason. On the other hand, when the imagination is stirred for all that is noble and right, its capacity to make the world a better place is enormous.

An illustration of the potency of this level of philosophy is a song that was sung years ago by a nine-year-old girl. It became the most requested song all over the country because it addressed a theme that did not require any logician for its defense. It touched the sensitivities of old and young in every strata of society.

> Dear Mr. Jesus, I just had to write to you
> Something really scared me, when I saw it on the news,
> A story 'bout a little girl beaten black and blue
> Jesus, thought I'd take this right to you. . . .
>
> Please don't let them hurt your children,
> We need love and shelter from the storm.
> Please don't let them hurt your children,
> Won't you keep us safe and warm.[5]

The reason for the effectiveness of this song is readily understood. Child abuse is one of those dastardly crimes that even a majority of criminals despise. In fact, child abusers often must be segregated to protect them from the avenging anger of prison mates. A belief this common, that you do not hurt a child, does not necessarily need a philosopher's help. The force of the incontrovertible truth, carried forth in the strains of a simple melody and made doubly persuasive through the voice of a child, can stir the imagination of a whole nation.

Why is this so? Imagine yourself caught in the middle of a conversation at a professors' luncheon, discussing the issue of child abuse. Imagine your reaction should you find that there were both protagonists and antagonists—some in favor of it, while others condemn it. It would stagger the imagination to think that some would defend the victimization of a child.

In fact, I put this theory to the test with some students at Oxford University who were seeking an answer to the question of evil. I asked a group of skeptics if I took a baby and sliced it to pieces before them, would I have done anything wrong? They had just denied that objective moral values exist. At my question, there was silence, and then, the lead voice in the group said, "I would not like it, but no, I could not say you have done anything wrong." My! What an aesthete. He would not like it. My! What irrationality—he could not brand it wrong. I only had to ask him that if evil is denied, what then remains of the original question?

Common sense alone dictates the rationale behind the protection and care of the most innocent and vulnerable of our society. Common sense also reveals that such a philosophy—"I would not like it but I could not say you've done anything wrong"—is *not livable* at the moment when one sees a knife thrust in his direction. And this is the point: While the appeal of the song above is to the imagination, it is the handmaiden of good sense and reason.

Samuel Taylor Coleridge expressed this very idea when he made a plea for the imagination, within the boundaries of reason, to play a vital role in the transmission of truth, as it pursued the good. And the lae English theologian Colin Gunton observed,

> Imagination understood in this way is not simply the mind's aimless and uncontrolled (Pavlovian) reaction to stimuli, but the way by which we are able to penetrate and indeed repeat after it, the very divine act of creation.[6]

Rightly understood and constructively used, imagination helps the mind pierce reality with unique glimpses through the inward eye. Wrongly understood and destructively used, imagination can become fertile ground for unmitigated evil. Its vulnerability lies in its inextricable link with our emotions and feelings, which can easily take off into fanciful flings. Unguarded feelings can in turn create a whole new set of absolutes, until reality is viewed as a dispensing machine, designed to submit to the whims of our fluctuating emotions. Imagination easily falls prey to what Canadian economist and humorist Stephen Leacock has said, "Many a man in love with a dimple makes the mistake of marrying the whole girl."[7]

Indeed, many individuals who take their emotions as a starting point for determining truth, in grabbing the finger of feeling, think they have grabbed the fist of truth. By thinking exclusively at this level, they are driven systematically further inward, until their whole world revolves around their personal passion with a dangerous self-absorption. They reshape their worldview to a "better felt than 'tellt' " perspective—if it feels good, do it; or as the line from the song says, "How can it be wrong when it feels so right?"

The history of modern cultures and their expressions easily demonstrate how the moods and indulgences of a nation have been generated by the popular writers, entertainers, and musicians of the day. Those who harness the strength of the arts mold the soul of a nation to an extraordinary degree, affecting and changing the way people think and act to drastic proportions. As the Scottish politician Andrew Fletcher (1655–1716) once noted, "Give me the making of the songs of a nation, and I care not who makes its laws."

This is a generation that listens with its eyes and thinks with its feelings.

Television and music media are such potent forces because they have within them the capacity to bypass reason and head straight for the imagination. They can bind the strongman of reason, and so capture the goods. Indeed, as I mentioned earlier, this is a generation that listens with its eyes and thinks with its feelings.

The existential philosophers of the 1950s and 1960s were fully aware of the imagination and the arts and used these avenues to impart a worldview of rebellion. Hence, the impact of artists and writers at this level of communication must be seen as continuous with moral philosophers. They enlarge the academic imagination, though they have a built-in aversion for systematization. They do not like to be put into categories. Since they address the here and now, they bear an obvious hostility to abstract theory, which to them obscures the roughness and untidiness of life. If life itself is so coarse and has such a jagged edge, why should a philosophy of life be uniform? They fail to see that they have made the effect the cause. They see life as a string of passions with which to conquer emptiness. The experience of feeling the here and now supercedes the existence of truth. To such people, experience precedes essence, the subjective overrules the objective, and what they do determines who they are. This inversion of thinking is what produces the grunts and groans of the gravediggers as they bury God. For, with his burial, all sense of life is buried. As they face the encroaching panic, they are forced to redefine everything, and each one has to create his own personal reality.

Level two appeals to the imagination and addresses why people live the way they live. In concert with reason it is immensely powerful for the cause of good. When it is allowed to run unchecked by reason in fitful responses to stimuli, such an approach ends up justifying even the most unconscionable acts.

Smuggling in Opinion

Level three, the third level of philosophy, is what I call "kitchen table conclusions." It is amazing how much of the moralizing and prescribing in life goes on during casual conversations. The settings can vary from sidewalk cafés, where frustrated philosophers pontificate on profound themes, to the kitchen table, where children interact with their parents on questions that deal with far-reaching issues. The question may arise out of the latest nagging news item or scandal of the day, or it could be a question raised in the classroom, such as, what would one do in a sinking boat with three life jackets and four passengers on board? This level of philosophizing escapes neither the beggar nor the academic dean of a prestigious school, because *why* is one of the earliest expressions of human life.

I recall an occasion when I had addressed a European university audience at an open forum that was chaired and moderated by a highly reputed scholar. The audience, recognizing his academic credentials and his great philosophical prowess, paid very close attention to what he said on some remote and obscure issues. They were in awe of him, even though much of what he said must have escaped the capacity of a large portion of the audience.

Shortly after this forum, we headed to his home, where he and his daughter got into a verbal sparring session over some evening plans she had made, the wisdom of which he had questioned. This discomforting conflict between father and daughter was a somewhat pitiful sight to see, for suddenly the accolades showered on him in the halls of learning a few moments earlier were distant and smothered echoes of an unimportant event.

What he believed and how he lived had come home and had given his daughter leverage to challenge his dictums for her. She was arrogating to herself the rights he could not deny on the basis of his

> *It was a pointed reminder to me that everything that I believe about life is sooner or later tested at the kitchen table, or in the family room, where young people are very quick to make applications on the basis of their parents' philosophy.*

own belief system. It was a pointed reminder to me that everything that I believe about life is sooner or later tested at the kitchen table, or in the family room, where young people are very quick to make applications on the basis of their parents' philosophy.

This is level three in action, for application has a biting reality to it. Yet on its own, such philosophizing lacks foundational authority and is merely an opinion that dares to prescribe without bothering to defend. It smuggles in an ethic while denying a moral referent.

Every individual makes moral judgments in his or her day-to-day interactions in life. It is the coinage by which we pay as we go. Without an accepted standard, a coin is worthless. The fundamental problem with level three, taken by itself, is that all denunciation implies a moral doctrine of some kind; and when morality cannot be justified, any denunciation ultimately undermines its own mines. Reality begs a better answer than mere applicative pronouncements.

Most talk shows are examples of conversation at level three, where the opinions thrown back and forth treat on an equal plane, sexuality and ice-cream parlors. Everything in this relativized culture becomes purely a matter of taste or preference.

One particular talk show host I know of has constantly and dogmatically favored abortion with no sympathy for the pro-life position. So uncompromising and extreme was his attitude that he refused to even take calls from men, saying that this particular subject had nothing to do with the male of the species. Not infrequently he would get into a tirade, vilifying those who opposed his position.

Very surprising, therefore, was his reaction to a newspaper article that described the process of preparation for some East European athletes before a competition. It explained that as part of their muscle development, they would plan to become pregnant two-to-three months before a key race. As the first two months of a pregnancy greatly enlarged the muscle capacity, they would reap its benefit and then abort the baby a few days before the race.

This article infuriated the talk show host, and he unsparingly denounced it as going to unpardonable limits. However, he never explained his own inconsistency. Prescriptivism is doomed as a starting point and can never justify itself. Level three deals with why one prescribes what he prescribes.

The Proper Way

To summarize, level one is supported by logic; level two is based on feeling; and level three is where all is applied to reality. To put it another way, level one states why we believe what we believe. Level two indicates why we live the way we live, and level three states why we legislate for others the way we do. For every life that is lived at a reasonable level, these three questions must be answered. First, can I defend what I believe in keeping with the laws of logic? That is, *is it tenable*? Second, if everyone gave himself or herself the prerogatives of my philosophy, could there be harmony in existence? That is, *is it livable*? Third, do I have a right to make moral judgments in the matters of daily living? That is, *is it transferable*?

None of these levels can live in isolation. They must follow a proper sequence. Here is the key: one must argue from level one, illustrate from level two, and apply at level three. Life must move from truth to experience to prescription. If either the theist or the atheist violates this procedure, he is not dealing with reality but creating one of his own.

Understanding these three levels uncovers the many-sided weaknesses of atheism. With feeling or experience as a starting point, life is not livable, because it will face contradiction on every side. Application as a starting point, without truth to support it, is only one step removed from feeling and cannot be justified. But when one starts with the truth, it can be proven in experience and be justifiably prescribed for others.

In this study of atheism we have seen the logical contradictions it embraces, the existential hell it creates, and the vacuous pronouncements it makes. This manifold vulnerability is what provoked the acerbic remark that atheism has a greater capacity to smell rotten eggs than to lay good ones, or to attack other systems than to defend its own.

APPENDIX
2

THE ESTABLISHMENT
OF A WORLDVIEW

*Few people have anything approaching an articulate
philosophy—at least as epitomized by the great philosophers. Even fewer, I suspect, have a carefully con-
structed theology. But everyone has a worldview. . . .
In fact, it is only the assumption of a worldview—
however basic or simple—that allows us to think at
all.*

—James Sire

We enter here into what may be legitimately called the
heart of the process; for failing here, we fail every-
where. The necessary ingredients that make up a
worldview are not thrown together in a haphazard fashion. Neither
are they composed tendentiously to fit a prejudiced conclusion.
Starting with self-evident statements, both direct and indirect, we
proceed to the establishment of a truth-centered worldview. When
that is established, it must meet certain tests to distinguish knowledge from mere opinion.

In *The Case for Christian Theism*, Arlie J. Hoover listed a number of necessary components for establishing a worldview. I shall mention five of them, and then add one more important aspect.

1. A good worldview will have a strong foundation in correspondence; it will have factual support. Conversely, it will refuse that which is known to be false. It must harness all areas of reality and not retain a selective sovereignty. To refuse to include facts that challenge the thesis or to arbitrarily make some subservient to others because they better fit a predetermined conclusion betrays a prejudice that distorts the worldview.

2. A good worldview should have a high degree of coherence or internal consistency. A logically contradictory system cannot be true. To be internally consistent it cannot have contradicting deductions, regardless of what "experiential needs" are met in the process.

Let me illustrate these two characteristics of correspondence and coherence. Some years ago I was able to witness a criminal trial involving child rape at the Old Bailey in London. The Old Bailey Courthouse has addressed some of the most publicized criminal cases in the history of London (Oscar Wilde was on trial there in 1895). The atmosphere was tense, filled with all of the attendant emotions—agony, anger, and drama. It became very clear that the attorneys were seeking to do two things. First, they wanted to bring either certainty or doubt into the allegations, depending upon the client they represented. Second, they wanted to determine how the alleged facts all fit together. They explored issues such as time and location by questioning witnesses, and with this wealth of information they tried to show either coherence or incoherence.

It was impossible to listen to these proceedings without realizing that truth could not stand on isolated statements: it had to fit the alleged story. Further, it was impossible to escape the fact that whichever way the judgment went, it would change the lives of the principals involved unalterably. Such a scenario, with all its implications, must be enacted scores of times every day in our world. The pursuit of correspondence to fact and the coherence of the whole, even in specific beliefs, cannot be expunged from the process of reaching accurate conclusions. This is true in court trials and in every other aspect of life.

3. A good worldview has explanatory power. The collation of facts leads to initial postulations, by which we devise our theories, our hypotheses, and then finally delineate our "laws." United facts and integrated deductions lead to systems. Facts ultimately do not just speak for themselves; they help build a theory, or provide the prescriptive elements, the eyeglasses, through which we view the world.

4. A good worldview will avoid two extremes. This means, said Hoover, that a good worldview will be neither too simple nor too complex. He uses the famous "Occam's razor test." William of Occam (1300–1349) supposedly said, "Do not multiply entities without necessity," which basically means that we are to resist the temptation to make our explanations too complex. If an explanation becomes too complex, Occam's razor will cut it off. On the other hand, an explanation should not become so simplistic that it commits the reductive fallacy. To make man an incomprehensible entity is to go to one extreme. To consider a man a mere brute is to reduce him to the other extreme. A good worldview, therefore, is neither too simple nor too complex in its explanatory power.

5. A good worldview has more than one line of evidence, not just one knockout argument. Cumulative evidence converges from several sources of data. Hoover's illustration of the metaphysician being like a good stage manager is excellent. One by one the manager clicks on a series of lights, placed at different angles around the stage. The full illumination from all the lights falls on the center of the stage. When all the lights are on, you should be able to see the manager's assertion in the center of the stage.[1]

To Hoover's five, I add this important sixth component.

6. A worldview is not complete in itself until it is able to refute, implicitly or explicitly, contrary worldviews. This is often a forgotten factor when arriving at a position. The law of noncontradiction (that a statement and its opposite cannot both be true) applies not only within a worldview but also between worldviews. Thus, it is more reasonable to say that all religions we know of are wrong than to assert that all are right. Any system that opens its arms wide enough to incorporate everything will end up strangling itself when the arms close in.

Most Eastern philosophers despise the law of noncontradiction, but they cannot shake its life-sized reality. The more they seek to assault the law of noncontradiction, the more it assaults them. For this very reason, and in recognition of its undeniability, an Eastern mystic said, "It is better to remain silent, for when the mouth opens, all are fools." The problem is that his mouth opened to tell

> *A worldview is not complete in itself until it is able to refute, implicitly or explicitly, contrary worldviews.*

us that. One may as well talk of a one-ended stick as to deny the law of noncontradiction.

Since our goal is to arrive at a worldview that meets these aforementioned tests, let me propose the approach that will accomplish that.

Human beings are unquestionably multisensory, or multifaceted, and the intimations of reality come to us from a diversity of sources. Therefore, it stands to reason that no one test will capture all of reality. The combination of several truth tests, harnessing their strengths and eliminating their weaknesses, would be the ideal path to take. This method is often called *combinationalism*, or systematic consistency, for it combines several methods to arrive at logical consistency, empirical adequacy, and experiential relevance.

In his book *Christian Apologetics*, Norman Geisler considered these three tests in combinationalism inadequate, unless preceded by two others, which he calls "unaffirmability as a test for falsity" and "undeniability as a test for truth." For readers who wish to pursue this, the reading would be well worth the effort. Geisler's reasoning is that systematic consistency is only appropriate within a worldview; it does not eliminate the possibility of other views being true. I think this judgment is merely the fine tuning of the process, because the threefold test of logical consistency, empirical adequacy, and experiential relevance ought to incorporate the unaffirmability and undeniability tests. For example, any system that denies the law of noncontradiction fails the test of logical consistency because while denying it, it affirms the law at the same time. In the same way, when one attempts to deny his existence he fails the test of experiential relevance because he is using his own existence to deny it. The undeniability and unaffirmability tests, whether seen separately from combinationalism or inherent within it, are crucial for truth testing and prevent any escape attempts of a worldview to deny reality.

The Final Approach

I have selected the combinational method because the defense of any position, sooner or later, finds itself ultimately in this terrain, reluctantly or otherwise. Winston Churchill, speaking of secretive war strategy, once said that the truth was so valuable that it had to be protected by a bodyguard of lies. This estimate applies to all of life's pursuits, though not always by intention. Truth is often avoided, or eludes us, because of a smokescreen of lies leading us the wrong way.

Let me use another analogy for a moment. Imagine a circle, with truth at the center, often hindered by a coarse periphery of resistance. Although various attempts are made to get to the center, entry is possible only by a certain approach. The closer one gets to the center, the more indispensable is systematic consistency. Even the revered Hindu philosopher Shankara, with his strong bent for a logic that is supposedly Eastern and his repeated attempts to elude the law of noncontradiction, nevertheless goes to great lengths to justify or offer his "cohesive" conclusions. The gravitational pull of the center makes consistency inescapable.

In summary, I frame my methodology in a three-four-five grid. The three tests (logical consistency, empirical adequacy, and expediential relevance) must be able to give truthful and consistent answers to the four questions of our origin, condition, salvation, and destiny. These four areas, in turn, will have to deal with five topics: God, reality, knowledge, morality, and humankind; or theology, metaphysics, epistemology, ethics, and anthropology. One may reverse this sequence and say that, on the basis of a study of these five areas, the answers to the four questions lie in the truth tests of the three components of systematic consistency. Then the conceptual framework, or the glasses through which we see this world, makes for a strong foundation in understanding reality and is able to deal with truth and error.[2]

NOTES

Chapter 1: Morticians of the Absolute

1. The original source from the *Dictionary of Quotations* is the *Seattle Daily Times*, May 7, 1962, 2. Gherman Titov: "Some say God is living here [in space]. I was looking around very attentively. But I did not see anyone there. I did not detect angels or gods. . . . I don't believe in God. I believe in man, his strength, his possibilities, and his reason."

2. Mortimer Adler, *The Synopticon: An Index to the Great Ideas*, vol. 1 (Chicago: Britannica, 1952), 543.

3. Stephen Hawking, *A Brief History of Time* (New York: Bantam Books, 1988).

4. On October 31, 1992, Pope John Paul II formally declared that Galileo was "not guilty" of the heresy charge brought against him by the Catholic Church.

5. Stanley Jaki, *The Road of Science and the Ways to God* (Edinburgh: Scottish Academic Press, 1986), 447.

6. Friedrich Nietzsche, in Faru Förster Nietzsche, *The Life of Nietzsche*, vol. 2 (New York: Sturgis and Walton, 1921), 656.

7. The superman is the one who has organized the chaos of his passions, given style to his character, and become creative. Aware of life's terrors, he nevertheless affirms life without resentment. He is one who stands as a "this-wordly" antithesis to God. In her old age, Nietzsche's sister saw Hitler as the one who epitomized that Nietzschean ideal.

8. Friedrich Nietzsche, "The Gay Science," in *The Portable Nietzsche*, ed. and trans. Walter Kaufmann (New York: Viking, 1954), 125.

9. Bryan Magee, *The Great Philosophers* (London: BBC Books, 1987), 247.

10. Quotation from table of contents for story by Dick Lehr and Mitchell Zuckoff, "The Thrill Killers," *Reader's Digest* (August 2003), 3.

11. Ibid., 183.

12. Malcolm Muggeridge, *A Third Testament* (New York: Ballantine Books, 1983).

Chapter 2: Is There Not a Cause?

1. C. Bibby, *Scientist Extraordinary: Life and Scientific Work of Thomas Henry Huxley* (New York: Pergamom, 1972), 41.

2. T. H. Huxley, *Westminster Review* 17 (1860), 541–70.

3. Jaki, *Road of Science*, 282.

4. See, for example, the works of William Dembski and Michael Behe among others. Numerous other scientists who question the claims of Darwinism jointly signed the Ad Hoc Origins Committee Document, stating, "We think a critical re-evaluation of Darwinism is both necessary and possible." The document and signers can be found at Apologetics.org, http://www.apologetics.org/news/adhoc.html.

5. Mary Hesse, "Criteria of Truth in Science and Theology," *Religious Studies* 11 (1976): 385–400.

6. Charles Sherrington, *Man on His Nature* (London: Pelican Books, 1955), 187.

7. Gregor Mendel (1822–1884) was the first person to trace and describe this view of life-inherited traits in successive generations of living organisms.

8. R. J. Berry, *God and Evolution* (London: Hodder & Stoughton, 1988), 93.

9. The debate between "punctuated equilibrium" and the traditional phyletic gradualism, or synthetic theory, has prompted some very pertinent remarks. Stephen Jay Gould said, "All paleontologists know that the fossil record contains precious little in the way of intermediate forms; transitions between major groups are characteristically abrupt" ("Return of the Hopeful Monster," *Natural History* 86, no. 6 [1977]: 22–30). Elsewhere, he says in one of his regular columns in *Natural History*, "The extreme rarity of transitional forms in the fossil record persists as the trade secret of paleontology. The evolutionary trees that adorn our textbooks have only data at the tips and the nodes of their branches; the rest is inference, however reasonable, not the evidence of fossils," (*Natural History* 85, no. 5 [1977]: 14).

10. Berry, *God and Evolution*, 99.

11. Jaki, *Road to Science*, 287, 442.

12. Lesslie Newbigin, *Foolishness to the Greeks* (London: SPCK, 1986), 74.

13. George Beadle, "Address at the Chicago Sunday Evening Club," quoted in the *Chicago Daily News* (March 18, 1962).

14. Francis H. C. Crick, *Of Molecules and Men* (Seattle: University of Washington Press, 1966), 10.

15. Jacques Monod, *Chance and Necessity* (London: E. T. Collins, 1973), 10.

16. Ibid., 167.

17. John Polkinghorne, *One World* (London: SPCK, 1986), 79–80.

Chapter 3: Virtue in Distress

1. Stephen Crane, "A Man Said to the Universe," http://eir.library.utoronto.ca/rpo/display/poem582.html.

2. Nietzsche, *The Portable Nietzsche*, 515.

3. Monism is the name given to a group of views that stress the oneness, or unity of reality. While some are partial monists, Shankara was an absolute monist, and therefore believed that the Absolute is beyond the sphere of predication. Brahman is the *Ultimate Reality*; all else is non-being.

4. Peter Kreeft, *Three Philosophies of Life* (San Francisco: Ignatius Press, 1989), 17–18.

5. Alasdair MacIntyre, *After Virtue* (London: Duckworth, 1987), 2.

6. See, for example, David Limbaugh's well-researched indictment of the secular elite's attempt to eradicate the influence of Christianity from public schools in his book *Persecution: How Liberals Are Waging War Against Christianity* (Washington, D.C.: Regnery, 2003).

7. Bertrand Russell, *Why I Am Not a Christian* (London: Unwin Books, 1967), 146.

8. Frederick W. H. Myers, *Criticisms and Interpretations*, Bartleby.com, http://www.bartleby.com/309/1001.html.

9. Paul Johnson, *Intellectuals* (New York: Harper & Row, 1988), 246.

10. William Shirer, *The Rise and Fall of the Third Reich: A History of Nazi Germany* (New York: Simon & Schuster, 1960), 100.

11. Adolf Hitler, in Norman Geisler, "Wretched Refuse," *Kindred Spirit*, August 1988.

12. Charles Darwin, "Letter to N. Gray, June 5, 1861," in *Life and Letters of Charles Darwin*, ed. Francis Darwin (1888, repr; New York: Basic Books, 1959), 2:374.

13. Darwin, "Letter to W. Graham, June 3, 1881," in *Life and Letters*, 1:316.

14. G. K. Chesterton, *As I Was Saying*, ed. Robert Knille (Grand Rapids: Eerdmans, 1984), 267.

15. Robert E. Fitch, "The Obsolescence of Ethics," *Christianity and Crisis: A Journal of Opinion* 19, no. 19 (November 16, 1959), 163–65.

16. Johnson, *Intellectuals*, 251. Dr. Norman Geisler has presented what is considered to be good evidence that Jean Paul Sartre became a theist in his last days; see his book *Is Man the Measure? An Evaluation of Contemporary Humanism* (Grand Rapids: Baker Books, 1983), 46.

17. Johnson, *Intellectuals*, 342.

18. William Shakespeare, *The History of Troilus and Cressida*, quoted in Richard Weaver, *Ideas Have Consequences* (Chicago: University of Chicago Press, 1984), 39.

19. J. P. Stern, quoted in Magee, *The Great Philosophers*, 242.

Chapter 4: Sisyphus on a Roll

1. T. S. Eliot, "Choruses from 'The Rock,' " *The Complete Poems and Plays of T. S. Eliot* (London: Faber & Faber, 1989), 147.
2. Voltaire, *Candide* (New York: Bantam, 1967), 97.
3. Paul Waitman Hoon, *Integrity of Worship* (Nashville: Abingdon, 1971), 30. Hoon fuses his thoughts on the subject with those of Langdon Gilkey to express this tension between freedom and bondage.
4. *The Oxford English Dictionary* cites the first written instance of the word *boredom* as occurring in 1852.
5. Chesterton, *As I Was Saying*, 265.
6. Samuel Taylor Coleridge, in Rupert Christiansen, *Romantic Affinities* (London: Sphere Books, 1988), 66.
7. James Simpson, in Peter Masters, *Men of Destiny* (London: The Evangelical Times, 1968), 36.

Chapter 5: Grave Doubts

1. William James, "The Sick Soul," in *The Varieties of Religious Experience*, ed. Martin E. Marty (New York: Penguin Books, 1982), 163.
2. Bertrand Russell, "A Free Man's Worship," *Mysticism and Logic and Other Essays* (London: Allen & Unwin, 1963), 41.
3. Malcolm Muggeridge, *Conversion* (Glasgow: William Collins Sons & Co. Ltd., 1988), 62.
4. Alfred Lord Tennyson, "In Memoriam A.H.H.," in *The Norton Anthology of English Literature*, 3rd ed., ed. M. H. Abrams (1975; repr. New York: W. W. Norton & Co., 2004), 55:2, 56:1–7.
5. William Wordsworth, "We Are Seven," ibid., 1367–69.
6. Winston Churchill, "The Grand Alliance," *Who Said What When* (London: Bloomsbury, 1988), 249.
7. Source and author unknown.

Chapter 6: Climbing in the Mist

1. C. S. Lewis, *Surprised by Joy* (New York: Harcourt, 1956), 228–29.
2. Colin Gunton, *Enlightenment and Alienation* (London: Marshall, Morgan & Scott, 1985), 11.
3. For anyone desiring specific definitions and detailed descriptions of these categories, I would recommend Norman Geisler's book *Christian Apologetics* (Grand Rapids: Baker Books, 1976).
4. See chapter 3, "The Anatomy of Faith" in Arlie J. Hoover, *Dear Agnos: Letters to an Agnostic in Defense of Christianity* (Joplin, MO: College Press Publishing Company, 1992), http://members.core.com/~tony233/Dear_Agnos.htm.
5. Descartes himself had a rather interesting approach to the senses. Starting from the vantage point of rational certainty, he argued for the existence of God.

Having established that argument, he felt God would not be a deceiver and argued for the existence of an eternal world on that theistic basis.

6. Albert Einstein, *Ideas and Opinions* (London: Souvenir Press, 1973), quoted in Lesslie Newbigin, *The Gospel in a Pluralistic Society* (London: SPCK, 1989), 29.

7. If the reader desires a rigorous argumentation for theism, I recommend Norman Geisler's *Christian Apologetics* or *Philosophy of Religion*. J. P. Moreland's *Scaling the Secular City* combines superb scholarship in argument and counterargument fashion. In addition, see William Lane Craig, *Reasonable Faith: Christian Truth and Apologetics* (Wheaton, IL: Crossway, 1994). Craig has also participated in two excellent debates: "What Is the Evidence For/Against the Existence of God?" (with outspoken atheist Peter Atkins) and "Does God Exist?" (with renowned atheistic philosopher Anthony Flew). Both debates are available on video through Ravi Zacharias International Ministries in Atlanta; www.rzim.org. For my purpose, I will not enter into that field because the nature of argumentation involved is more appropriately handled in a textbook than it is in an effort such as this dealing with the existential struggles for meaning. Ideally, these two different approaches complement one another. For this reason I recommend these resources as further study for a complete view of the arguments in defense of theism.

8. See Ronald N. Nash, *Faith and Reason* (Grand Rapids: Zondervan, 1988), 33.

9. George MacDonald, *The Curate's Awakening* (Minneapolis: Bethany House, 1985), 161.

10. Richard Weaver, *Ideas Have Consequences* (Chicago: University of Chicago Press, 1984), 19.

Chapter 7: With Larger Eyes Than Ours

1. C. S. Lewis has a strong point, arguing for the universe itself as a miracle. "If the 'natural' means that which can be fitted into a class, that which obeys a norm, that which can be paralleled, that which can be explained by other events, then Nature herself, as a whole, is *not* natural. If a miracle means that which must simply be accepted, the unanswerable actuality which gives no account of itself but simply *is* then the universe is one great miracle" (*God in the Dock* [Grand Rapids: Eerdmans, 1970], 36, Lewis's emphasis).

2. Colin Gunton, *Enlightenment and Alienation* (London: Marshall, Morgan & Scott, 1985), 48.

3. Robert Jastrow, *God and the Astronomers* (New York: Warner Books, 1978), 105.

4. Chesterton, *As I Was Saying*, 267.

5. J. Morley, *Life of Gladstone*, vol. 3, 535, quoted in *Making Moral Decisions*, ed. D. M. MacKinnon (London: SPCK, 1969), 48.

6. Joseph Fletcher, *Situation Ethics* (Philadelphia: Westminster Press, 1966), 77.

7. Iris Murdoch, *The Sovereignty of Good* (London: ARK Pub., 1989), 80.

8. Alexander Pope, "An Essay on Criticism," *Who Said What When* (London: Bloomsbury, 1988), 125.

9. Alexis de Tocqueville, *Voyage en Angleterre et en Irlande,* May 18, 1835.

10. Paul Johnson, *Modern Times* (New York: Harper & Row, 1983), 428.

11. Bernard Shaw, preface to "Imprisonment," *English Local Government,* quoted in *Making Moral Decisions,* ed. D. M. MacKinnon (London: SPCK, 1969), 67.

12. Reinhold Niebuhr, *Moral Man and Immoral Society* (London: SCM Press, 1963), 265–66.

13. From a debate between Dennis Prager and Jonathan Glover, "Can We Be Good without God?" Oxford University, March 3, 1993, included in *Ultimate Issues,* vol. 9, no. 1. This debate is available at http://www.dennisprager.com.

14. Alfred Lord Tennyson, "In Memoriam A.H.H.," 119, 124:11–15.

15. Lee Iacocca, *Talking Straight* (New York: Bantam, 1988), 35.

16. Rudolph Bultmann, in Gunton, *Enlightenment and Alienation,* 92.

17. For further comparison of Freud and Christianity (through the lenses of C. S. Lewis), see Dr. Armand M. Nicholi's fascinating book *The Question of God: C. S. Lewis and Sigmund Freud Debate God, Love, Sex, and the Meaning of Life* (New York: The Free Press, 2002).

18. Francis Thompson, "The Hound of Heaven," http://eir.library.utoronto.ca/rpo/display/poem2204.html.

19. G. Wade Robinson, "I Am His and He Is Mine."

20. T. S. Eliot, "Little Gidding," in *T. S. Eliot, The Complete Poems and Plays* (London: Faber & Faber, 1989), 197.

21. Malcolm Muggeridge, *Jesus Rediscovered* (Garden City, NY: Doubleday, 1969), 77.

22. Thomas Merton, *Seeds of Contemplation* (New York: New Directions, 1949).

23. Will Durant, *Caesar and Christ* (New York: Simon & Schuster), 602.

24. For those who would like to pursue the cumulative and persuasive evidence of the resurrection of Jesus Christ, there are many excellent books. They deal with both biblical and extrabiblical evidence. I mention just a few here. Though written several years ago, the following books are considered classics and are well worth tracking down. R. T. France, *The Evidence for Jesus* (Downers Grove, IL: InterVarsity, 1986); John Warwick Montgomery, *History and Christianity* (Downers Grove, IL: InterVarsity, 1965); Frank Morison, *Who Moved the Stone?* (Grand Rapids: Zondervan, 1958); Terry L. Miethe, ed., *Did Jesus Rise from the Dead? The Resurrection Debate* (San Francisco: Harper & Row, 1989). In the Miethe source the two debaters are Gary Habermas and Anthony Flew.

25. C. S. Lewis, *The Lion, the Witch and the Wardrobe* (London: William Collins Sons & Co., 1950), chap. 15.

26. Chesterton, "The Convert," in *As I Was Saying,* 25.

27. Paul W. Hoon, *Integrity of Worship* (Nashville: Abingdon, 1971), 141.

28. Don Wyrtzen and L. E. Singer, "Finally Home."

29. Blaise Pascal, "Section III: Of the Necessity of the Wager" in *Pensées*, trans. W. F. Trotter (1660; trans. 1907; Christian Classics Ethereal Library, 1997), http://www.ccel.org/p/pascal/pensees/pensees04.htm.

30. Pascal, *Pensées*, chap. XII, 434.

Appendix 1: The Finger of Truth and the Fist of Reality

1. C. S. Lewis, "Learning in War-Time," in *The Weight of Glory* (San Francisco: HarperSanFransico, 1980), 59.

2. Ambrose Bierce, *The Devil's Dictionary*, chap. 13, excerpt 54 (New York: Oxford University Press, 1999), 134.

3. Somerset Maugham, *The Summing Up* (New York: Viking Press, 1938).

4. Peter Kreeft, *Three Philosophies of Life* (San Francisco: Ignatius, 1989), 54.

5. Words and music to "Dear Mr. Jesus" by Richard Klender. Song performed by Sharon Batts. See http://www.richardklender.com/ and http://DayOfTheChild.org.

6. Colin Gunton, *Enlightenment and Alienation* (London: Marshall, Morgan & Scott, 1985), 33.

7. Stephen Leacock, *Literary Lapses* (London: J. Lane; New York: John Lane Company, 1911), BrainyQuote, http://www.brainyquote.com/quotes/quotes/s/stephenbl105033.html.

Appendix 2: The Establishment of a Worldview

1. Arlie J. Hoover, *The Case for Christian Theism* (Grand Rapids: Baker Books, 1976), 52.

2. Ronald Nash in *Faith and Reason* rightly considered these as needful for a worldview study.

Ravi Zacharias has spoken in countries worldwide and in numerous universities, notably Harvard, Cambridge, and Princeton. He received his Master of Divinity from Trinity Evangelical Divinity School and was a visiting scholar at Cambridge University. He has been conferred with three honorary doctorates.

Dr. Zacharias is well versed in the disciplines of comparative religions, cults, and philosophy, and he held the chair of evangelism and contemporary thought at Alliance Theological Seminary for three and a half years. He has written numerous books and is heard weekly on the radio program *Let My People Think*.

Dr. Zacharias is president of Ravi Zacharias International Ministries, headquartered in Atlanta, Georgia, with additional offices in Canada, India, Singapore, the United Arab Emirates, and the United Kingdom. He is married to Margie, and they have three grown children.